CONSTRAINT AND VARIETY
IN AMERICAN EDUCATION

David Riesman is Professor of Social Sciences at the University of Chicago, where he has been since 1946, and will become Henry Ford II Professor of Social Sciences at Harvard University in September 1958. He was originally trained as a lawyer, and upon graduation from Harvard Law School became law clerk to Justice Brandeis and later deputy assistant district attorney of New York County. He was also a teacher of law at the University of Buffalo from 1937 to 1941.

An abridged edition of *The Lonely Crowd* and *Selected Essays from Individualism Reconsidered*, other works by Professor Riesman, also appear in the Anchor series. CONSTRAINT AND VARIETY IN AMERICAN EDUCATION was first published in 1956.

DAVID RIESMAN

CONSTRAINT AND VARIETY IN AMERICAN EDUCATION

WITH A NEW PREFACE

BY THE AUTHOR

DOUBLEDAY ANCHOR BOOKS

DOUBLEDAY & COMPANY, INC.

GARDEN CITY, NEW YORK

1958

COVER AND TYPOGRAPHY BY EDWARD GOREY

Reprinted by arrangement with the
University of Nebraska Press

Library of Congress Catalog Card Number 58–6648

Copyright © 1956, 1958 by the University of Nebraska Press

Printed in the United States of America

Dedicated to
Everett Cherrington Hughes

CONTENTS

The idea of progress, illustrated by contrasting the
confidence in right reason of a nineteenth-century
educator (Andrew D. White) with the unsureness
of a group of harassed school superintendents today, pp. 169–171; nevertheless, despite recent erosions, there is now more protection for professional
attitudes in the schools and colleges than ever before, and less social conventionality of the sort
Veblen satirized, pp. 172–173; a return to the
theme at the beginning, that education in its topmost reaches suffers from attainment of goals, pp.
173–174

CONSTRAINT AND VARIETY
IN AMERICAN EDUCATION

PREFACE TO THE ANCHOR EDITION

These lectures were given to students and faculty at the University of Nebraska, and then published by the University of Nebraska Press in a limited edition; they represent a preliminary attempt to deal with an immense range of problems about which my knowledge is still spotty. Since the lectures were written, I am seeking to learn more about the country's gamut of institutions of higher learning, thanks in part to a grant from the Carnegie Corporation.

What I am learning confirms my view that the problems dealt with in these Nebraska lectures matter very much, and confirms my hope that what I have to say may stimulate further discussion, research, and understanding. In preparing this edition, I have made only insignificant corrections. But I feel that a few points require additional emphasis, and want to turn to them.

In the lectures, I make an occasional remark about "consumer research" in education, referring both to students' finding out which are the "best" colleges and to the increasingly influential work of high-school guidance personnel. The more I have considered the matter, the more I have become convinced that the cause of improved education would be enormously aided if some impartial yet fearless agency could issue vivid and candid reports on colleges and schools of the sort Consumers Union publishes on commodities. It is astonishing, when one thinks about it, that the FTC polices advertising for hard goods where often the worst that can happen is that one can be cheated of money, and that various consumer-research organizations provide reliable data on vacuum cleaners, driers, radios, and canned goods, while no similiar agency polices school and college catalogues and brochures and does research on the qualitative aspects of education from the student's point of view. If one loses a few dollars through misleading advertising, one can make others, but if one loses four years through misleading schooling, one cannot make them up—on the contrary, in some cases, one may have formed false values, false estimates of one's self, of others, and of the universe.

To be sure, there are the accrediting agencies, which operate with respect to colleges on a regional basis. They serve, or so it can be argued, to raise the floor by requiring certain minima: books in the library, Ph.D.s on the faculty. These minima are not to be sneered at—though, like other observers of the educational scene, I have visited nonaccredited colleges that are far superior to some accredited ones (some of the latter indeed produce graduates who are barely literate). Moreover, through published data one can get some evidence for a judgment about the academic quality of a relatively small number of the thousand accredited colleges in this country; but to interpret this material in terms of the problem of matching a particular student, with only partially discovered potentialities, to a particular college, also with only partially discovered potentialities, is exceedingly difficult. Thus, there exist several excellent studies done at Wesleyan which report the proportion to total graduates of scientists and scholars produced at a number of colleges, providing in this way one yard-stick for over-all excellence.[1] In the first of these, *Origins of American Scientists*, vignettes are presented of the scholarly quality of several dozen colleges, including such well-known ones as Haverford, Oberlin, and Williams, and such little-known ones as Hope and Linfield, in terms of the influences favoring and retarding the development of scientific vocations in their student bodies. Similarly, for colleges which are members of the College Entrance Examination Board (less than a quarter of all accredited institutions), scores exist comparing their entering classes on academic performance with national norms; and high-school guidance counselors have access to these figures (and to a profile of the geographic and other distributions of students), although students and parents seem not to. So, too, in his Teacher Apprehension Study, Professor Lazarsfeld developed "quality indices" for various types of colleges on the basis both of published data of the sort used in accreditation (e.g., number of books in the library per student) and of data concerning the scholarly record of the social scientists interviewed in his own survey; but this material, gathered under promise of anonymity, can only be used to sort colleges by types, not individually.

Thus, data is publicly available for only a limited number of institutions, and even then it is often out of date (for example, the material in *Origins of American Scientists* relates largely to the period before the Second World War). Moreover, the question of what is "qual-

[1] See Robert H. Knapp and H. B. Goodrich, *Origins of American Scientists* (Chicago: University of Chicago Press, 1952), and Knapp and Joseph J. Greenbaum, *The Younger American Scholar: His Collegiate Origins* (Chicago: University of Chicago Press, 1953); and, for a discussion of types of college and the problem of comparison, Natalie Rogoff, *Board Member Colleges: A Comparative Analysis*, an unpublished study prepared for the College Entrance Examination Board, by the Bureau of Applied Social Research, Columbia University (1957).

ity" remains elusive: it refers to a complex of variables and, as indicated in my first lecture, no single scale suffices. Correspondingly, the various books I have seen which purport to guide prospective students are not very helpful. The *Handbook* put out by the College Entrance Examination Board includes brief statements by member colleges which, like much catalogue material, is most illuminating to those who already know how to interpret institutional advertising; and commercial handbooks (such as Lovejoy's) are about as useful as most booklets prepared by chambers of commerce for prospective tourists.

Not that all students or their parents are notably eager for intelligent guidance. John P. Netherton, Associate Dean of Students at the University of Chicago, once described for me the annual "college day" which the high schools of a certain Midwestern city sponsor. There is a meeting in a big hall at which the various college representatives put up desks while high-school youngsters and their parents come in and, as it were, shop around. Some colleges seek to lure the customers with flossy booklets, and the tone of the event was summed up for Dean Netherton in the incident of a father's picking up one such booklet and shouting across the room to his daughter: "Hey, Janie, come here. They have sailing at this college!" Just as consumer-research publications have a relatively small circulation, so one would expect that a similar publication concerning colleges would aim for and reach only the more alert and potentially discriminating, while great numbers of families would continue to choose colleges much as they choose cars or clothes: on the basis of student grapevine or neighbors' gossip ("opinion leadership") reinforced by advertising, or on the basis of family tradition or of a search for the prestige of a new tradition.

Honest and probing consumer research is, however,

useful to the "producer" as well as to the consumer. Not only does it help to reveal faults as others see them (something colleges attempt on occasion through "self-studies" or the use of outside experts), but it serves to bring changes in a program or curriculum to people's attention. Advertising in the college field is, of course, limited to some degree by professional ethics, so that reputable institutions may announce a new set of courses in American studies or a strengthened faculty in statistics in the Sunday *New York Times* and the professional journals; but of course they do not buy time on television or even a page in *The Saturday Review*; nor is there any ready way for them to announce changes in their admissions policies or in their patterns of recruitment that have made the college a more intellectual or artistic milieu. Thus, the market for new students—and, indeed, for new faculty—is often inelastic; that is, the quality of a school changes faster than its clientele recognizes; and colleges that have developed a novel or more demanding program cannot get the students to match it, while other institutions that have decayed cannot keep away students who should no longer go there. While autos carry their advertising, so to speak, on their body shells, which speak as loudly as print or TV commercials, colleges can change inside their shells with hardly anyone's noticing. And the result can be tragic, not only for misled students, but for imaginative faculty and administrators who may not live long enough to be rewarded by the appearance of good students attracted by those changes.

Let me take the present situation of Amherst College for an example (I may not be accurate in all details, but the main outlines are clear and could be duplicated elsewhere). The courageous imagination which Alexander Meiklejohn brought to the institution did not entirely vanish when he was forced out by "home guarders" (see pp. 36–39) among the entrenched faculty, alumni, and trustees in 1924: in the 1930s and since, the college has brought liberal and spirited men to the faculty, and recently President Charles Cole has appointed a number of distinguished men (including Henry Steele Commager, Alfred Kazin, and Donald McKay) to raise still further the community's level of learning. For a number of years, the required curriculum of the first two years has been a real challenge even to well-prepared students: they meet in English, in science, and in their introduction to American civilization a set of high and invigorating demands. The college has, of course, like other good schools at the present time, many times more applicants than it can accept, and it is beginning to draw some who are aware of what it has to offer the exceptionally able student. Even so, there are still not enough applicants who sufficiently differentiate today's Amherst from a composite Ivy League image: they may lump it indiscriminately with Williams or Bowdoin or Dartmouth. And of course such judgments tend to be self-confirming; for students who could profit from a place like Amherst do not always know about it.

Indeed, I suspect that students in college are in some measure taken in by the stereotypes that led them there, so that they do not discover and therefore help create the degree of stimulation their setting might allow. To be sure, since their choice was largely irrational in the first instance, they will tend to justify it retroactively by fervent alumni loyalty, based on selective perception of "their" colleges. This loyalty in turn, of course, makes it more difficult for an institution to alter its public image, save where a provocative president makes a frontal assault upon it. Likewise, the "drummers" whom the colleges send out are themselves often unaware of developments which may be of great importance to a few unusual prospective students, but which cannot readily be summarized and sold. Since, as I remark in these lectures, good teachers need good students to keep them good, it frequently happens that a college almost accumulates that "critical mass" requisite for a profound alteration in its image and in its impact on students, and then loses the opportunity to create the impact because not enough students of the right sort come at the right time.

I need hardly illustrate the many cases of the opposite sort, where a college coasts on its reputation and where its clientele is ignorant of the fact that it isn't what it used to be—or, more probably, that what it used to be is no longer adequate for today. Such coasting disheartens those who would like to see the college develop, since it encourages the complacency of the home guard; and of course also cheats the students who come expecting that college will be different from high school, when in fact it may only be more of the same, or worse. The history of American higher education is full of instances of leading institutions that have gone to seed, without any bankruptcy receiver's coming in—precisely because the customers, attracted by the brand name, do keep coming in.

A moment's thought makes it apparent that college criticism is enormously more difficult than commodity criticism (though the latter, too, is more difficult than it appears to consumer researchers who reduce all values to a narrow functionalism). There are a thousand accredited colleges, some of them changing so fast as to be more like perishables than like hard goods. They have to be examined on the spot, not in a central laboratory, and where is one to find the examiners who can get hold of the relevant information, protect their sources, treat matters with a broad comparative perspective, and develop confidence in the good faith and good sense of the agency for which they work? As my colleague, Dean Netherton, has observed, such an agency might best begin by instructing students in what to look for in visiting a college, reading its brochures, and talking with its emissaries, much as the consumer magazines tell their readers how to buy clothes or a used car. Still, I think it conceivable that, with enough planning and inventiveness, a respected clearinghouse for penetrating reports on colleges could be created.

To be sure, there is some danger that, if consumer reports were to become the exclusive source of recruitment—a most unlikely prospect!—the image of a college might become frozen at the level of its present state; today ignorance and poor feedback permit some colleges to recruit, as I have indicated, better students than they deserve, though these colleges may then for this very reason grow up to the students' expectations. Thus, reports on colleges would have to allow for possibilities of change—particularly if the student body is changing, since the quality of students is probably of more importance, other things being equal, than the quality of the staff.

Moreover, no one should underestimate the difficulty of finding out anything beyond routine data concerning the climates of sizable educational institutions. A large proportion of the faculty have a stereotype as to what their students are like which is often quite wide of the mark (and with, no doubt, some unconscious purposefulness, frequently self-defeating as well), and the more articulate students themselves are not always capable informants. The studies at Vassar that have recently been done under the Mellon Foundation's auspices show how intense and full must be any efforts to discover the varieties of student subculture, even at an apparently

rather homogeneous women's college,[2] and it is evident
that the anthropological and social-psychological techniques for investigations of this type remain, for the
most part, to be discovered. For this very reason, however, the demand for disinterested consumer research on
colleges would be of benefit not only to students and
faculty but also to our understanding of adolescence
generally; a great deal more is known about the so-
cialization of the child at home and at school in the
early years than about the impact of the years spent in
college, in the armed services, or on the first job.[3]

Nor should one underestimate the resistance colleges
would put up to this kind of investigation, even where
the results might be favorable to them. All the objec-
tions to the "newer" social sciences which I discuss in
the second lecture of this volume would arise against
"anthropological" studies of the college as a subculture
or series of subcultures. Academicians would rightly fear
that their professional standards, so painfully raised,
would be threatened by customer demands strengthened by techniques akin to market research. The fears
are all the more justified since students, though not the
only "customers" of a college (other customers include
the academic profession itself, intellectuals generally,
and future generations), can be the most parochial and
strident.

As just indicated, faculty members are themselves a
constituency, since they, too, are often attracted from

2 See the preliminary report by Nevitt Sanford, Mervin B.
Freedman, et al., in The Journal of Social Issues, vol. 12 (1956),
pp. 1–70.
3 Robert W. White's Lives in Progress (New York: Dryden
Press, 1952), based on observations of Harvard undergraduates
followed up during the early stages of their careers, is an illuminating indication of what might be attempted for other collegiate
settings, particularly when "anthropological" materials on the
campus culture can be combined with psychological profiles of
individuals.

one place to another by false appearances (including lack of knowledge of the possibilities at the institutions they are leaving). The faculty member who visits a place where he expects to get an appointment is seldom in a good position to make a judgment as to what sort of a climate he will find or help create, and he tends to move in terms of criteria of prestige rather than in terms, more complex to assess, of what opportunities he will have to develop as a scholar and a person. If he is any good, he is a lifelong student himself, and the knowledge meaningful to the more enterprising students would also be significant for him.

Still another constituency is the world of the foundations which make grants to institutions of higher education; some of them have what is perhaps the most valuable market-research information (now unavailable), for their officials make it their business to keep in touch with new developments and, in the best cases, maintain "sources" on the faculties much as a good journalist would do who was trying to cover the educational scene. (Yet at times it seems as if the foundations themselves are intimidated from using the knowledge they have, so strong are the lobbies of the entrenched educational powers on the one hand, and the foundations' need to get rid of annual income diplomatically on the other.)

I have no good answer, however, to someone who says that colleges are already too much caught up in our competitive patterns of culture (something these lectures themselves attest) and that consumer research, no matter how carefully done, would only strengthen the tendency among college administrations and faculties towards isomorphism, towards taking each other as models rather than developing new and risky forms. Just as market research convinced the Chrysler Corporation that its cars, to reach a wider market, would have to look like General Motors cars, only more so, so comparative studies of colleges might only reinforce the crassly expansionist mood from which higher education already suffers. Argument concerning programs would then, even more than at present, be couched in public-relations terms, rather than in terms of somebody's conviction as to what is a good education, even if the students or the wider publics aren't aware of it. Precisely such misgivings as to the application of false standards of judgment, once consumers are too much taken into account, operate to prevent hospitals from publishing widely their morbidity rates, law firms their batting averages of cases won and lost (district attorneys running for office do sometimes publicize their rate of convictions—usually with mercy and justice quietly losing out), or colleges the median income, numbers in Who's Who, or divorce rates of their graduates. If there is any solution to this dilemma of applying competitive lay standards to "businesses" run not for profit, it must be in the direction of substituting a somewhat more open and objective inter-academic competition for the covert competition that now goes on. For open competition is surely better than the present intended or chaotic ignorance as to what is perhaps the most important decision that families make (more important, often, than their choice of suburb) because of the fear that better information more equally distributed will be disruptive of the control colleges now have over certain "territories" by custom, grapevine, and high-school guidance routines.[4]

4 For discussion of some of the issues involved in matching students and colleges, cf. B. Alden Thresher, "A Problem in Communication," *The College Board Review*, vol. 23 (1954), pp. 439–443; and Frank H. Bowles, "Candidates and Confusions," *College and University*, vol. 32, pp. 467–480.

These considerations make it evident that the problem of consumer research on educational institutions is part of a broader issue: how can we get adequate consumer research on *services*, not commodities, as our society increasingly spends its surplus on them—on education, medicine, recreation, government, psychotherapy, and advice of all sorts. Professional bodies police their membership to some extent—and fend off the too critical or too credulous lay publics. What gets lost is the problem of matching a specific professional to a specific client, especially since many professional people are inclined to feel themselves suited to anyone who comes (within the limits of their special competence) and not to notice subtle and idiosyncratic factors that make for good or awkward matching. It is, of course, the same with colleges which may be "good" in general, yet not good for a particular student who would do better elsewhere. What is at stake here is not minimum protection but maximum advantage, and the professions and service trades in this country have not kept up with the increased expectations that their very achievements have invited. Thus, even a far better college than one's parents attended may dishearten the more mature and demanding college generation of today.

This growth in expectations may be one element in the dismal pattern of collegiate failure disclosed by a study which at least makes a stab at organizing existing consumer research on colleges; I refer to Philip Jacob's *Changing Values in College*, a report to the Edward Hazen Foundation. Professor Jacob has re-examined the various investigations of the impact of colleges on their graduates and the impact of particular professors or programs, and he has come up with conclusions not too different from those set forth in these lectures, namely that college makes the great majority of its denizens

more tolerant and cosmopolitan but hardly alters them
in any fundamental way (with the exception of a few
institutions like Antioch, Haverford, St. John's, Harvard, Wesleyan, Reed that confront the student with
something radically different from what he has had in
high school). While one might quarrel with his interpretations—and undoubtedly, as already indicated, we
lack adequate methods for assessing change in adolescence and for assigning it to one or another factor in a
complex culture—the Jacob report has jolted the complacency of a good many officials who had at least hoped
that their institutions meant something to the students
who passed through them. It is doubtful whether consumer research of the sort I have here recommended
would turn up more damning over-all evidence than the
Jacob report already has assembled; it might on the contrary serve to differentiate his findings and thus to
encourage the institutions which do mean something
and further shake those which don't.

One such differentiation would involve closer attention to the students of potential thoughtfulness and
moral purpose (not necessarily the ablest as conven-
tionally graded and defined), for it is these students
who could not only benefit most by perceptive matching
with an appropriate academic setting but could also help
to color that setting as the other students experience it.
In spite of all the concern presently being voiced about
the gifted student, and in spite of the ability of the more
popular colleges to set increasingly high standards for
entrance, it is my impression that it is precisely the better students at the better colleges who are often disap-
pointed today; as described in the first of my lectures,
they find their teachers "one-up" on them in academic
knowledge, but seldom genuinely interested in challenging them as persons or touching them closely in

terms of their whole conception of life or of the world. Indeed, most professors conceive of themselves today as having quite a different function, while those few who do try to interest their students in the great problems most often report that the new "found generation" is uninvolved where not consciously apathetic. I am inclined to think that this verdict is unfair to young people and that they can be moved if one begins by listening and not being too easily put off by surface self-protection and cynicism.

Still, it seems to me unlikely that the present generation of teachers will cross the generational gap or care enough about the human fate of their students to risk rebuff and despair. Thus, the expectations the more sensitive students may develop will probably not be met, save in rare and often chance encounters. If so, higher education will continue to get bigger and better without getting better enough. Accordingly an alternating current of hope and despair runs through my three lectures, in which I conclude that on the whole the colleges in this country have improved enormously in the last generation, but insufficiently so to match what we now should expect of them.

The same, I believe, can be said of the American experience itself, of which the schools and colleges are such a symptomatic refraction: our hopes for a better, more humane quality of life have risen even faster than our national income. That, at any rate, is how I interpret those critics of my lectures who found them too complacent, in the light of their own observations of contemporary education.[5] We have no standard based

---

[5] Cf. the discerning reviews to this effect by Goodwin Watson, *Teachers College Record*, vol. 58 (1957), pp. 283–284; and David M. Schneider, *American Anthropologist*, vol. 59 (October 1957), pp. 904–906.

on Europe or on our past performance by which to judge progress or regression in educational matters, for our present situation renders both our own and Europe's past obsolete for comparative purposes. And if my critics tell me that our institutions of higher education lack aliveness and are neither truly critical nor truly creative, I can only agree and add that this is true of our country as a whole: we lack even the goals that would inspire us to more discriminating expectations and more relevant dissatisfactions.

Thus on reflection I must qualify the judgment which appears at the end of my first lecture where I say that "I am somewhat more impressed with the self-renewing tendencies in academia than depressed by complacent success and mindless stagnation." I still believe that this is true enough, if one thinks, for instance, of the stagnation Veblen described in his *The Higher Learning in America* or that is pictured in the college novels of the '20s; academic competition moves at a quickened pace and faculties are less somnolent (if perhaps slightly more careerist) than they once were. However, as I have just said, all such comparisons are beside the point when one looks, not at where we've been, but at where we're going: into a virtually opaque future which no longer appears in the least utopian, even to science-fiction writers. In all probability, neither our educational nor our other institutions will have too much bearing on that future: in very large part they incorporate enough of it to seem up-to-date but, as the lectures indicate, it is the up-to-dateness of fashion rather than of liberating invention.

Still, I am an educator, and I cannot help working for the improvement of education, for the sake of that minority which can be moved by it, no matter what portends for the nation and the planet. I am encouraged whenever I learn, as I often did in working on these lectures, of some increased vitality in a school system or a college; and there is a great deal of this, often in places that seem on the surface unpromising. For I believe, as I have elsewhere written, that one must live on two levels, that of practical reform and that of utopian vision, and in the dialectic between these levels, activity on the one may accompany temporary defeat on the other.

D.R.

Brattleboro, Vermont
May 1957

ACKNOWLEDGEMENTS

This book is developed from lectures given in the Humanities Series of the University of Nebraska in April 1956. It reflects a modest amount of research on secondary schools (cf. the discussion of private and public high schools in *Faces in the Crowd*) and colleges, mainly in the East and Middle West. It also reflects—as any writing on education can hardly help doing—my experiences as a student, first at a Friends' day school for boys in Philadelphia, and then at Harvard College and Law School, where I took an active part in proposals for educational reform. And of course I have learned a good deal about education from the program in general education at the College of the University of Chicago—a program that has brought a stream of visitors to examine our curriculum and to trade with us their own educational experience.[1] I have also drawn on the research and observation of others. Thus, I am especially indebted to the work of the man to whom this book is dedicated, Everett Cherrington Hughes, both to his in-

[1] Cf. my article, "Some Problems of a Course in 'Culture and Personality,'" *Journal of General Education*, vol. 5 (1951), pp. 122–136.

quiries into what might be called the "career" of institutions,[2] and to his study now underway at the University of Kansas Medical School—a study concerned with how medical school students learn to be doctors of various sorts; I am likewise indebted to studies of medical education directed by Professor Robert K. Merton of Columbia. I have profited from the studies of high schools in relation to community social structure sponsored by W. Lloyd Warner and Robert J. Havighurst.[3]

Recently I have had the opportunity to take a small part in a large-scale study of college teachers' apprehension, sponsored by the Fund for the Republic and directed by Professor Paul F. Lazarsfeld of Columbia.[4] I was thus enabled to visit a number of institutions as well as to make use of the interviews and other data gathered throughout the country.[5]

I have had the benefit of the criticisms of a number of friends, familiar with various aspects of education,

[2] Cf. his pamphlet, Cycles and Turning Points: The Significance of Initiation in Human Culture, published by the National Council of the Protestant Episcopal Church (no date).

[3] Cf. W. Lloyd Warner and Associates, Democracy in Jonesville (New York: Harper and Bros., 1949); August B. Hollingshead, Elmtown's Youth (New York: Wiley, 1949); Robert J. Havighurst and Hilda Taba, Adolescent Character and Personality (New York: Wiley, 1949); and notably W. Lloyd Warner, Robert J. Havighurst, and Martin B. Loeb, Who Shall Be Educated? (New York: Harper and Bros., 1944).

[4] Cf. Lazarsfeld and Wagner Thielens, The Academic Mind: Social Scientists in a Time of Crisis (Glencoe, Ill.: The Free Press, 1958), as well as forthcoming publications edited by Professor Lazarsfeld.

[5] For analysis of this material and many useful criticisms of these lectures, I am indebted to Mark Benney, Elizabeth Drake, and June Sachar; funds for the analysis were provided in part by the Fund for the Republic, in part by the Foundations' Fund for Research in Psychiatry (under whose auspices Mr. Benney and I have been studying forms of communication in research and polling interviews).

who read one or more of the lectures in earlier versions.[6]
Several are referred to in footnotes; here I want to ac-
knowledge particularly helpful suggestions from: Bernard Bailyn, Richard Hofstadter, and Richard J. Storr,
historians, *inter alia*, of education; Louis Harris, of the
survey research firm of Louis Harris and Associates, who
took part in the initial phases of the Teacher Apprehension Study; Paul F. Lazarsfeld (to whom I am indebted
for many stimulating ideas in addition to the opportunity to make use of material gathered by him in the
study referred to above); Arnold A. Rogow (also for access to his study of school-board politics); Arthur J.
Brodbeck (also for access to a study of what is "controversial" in high school teaching); Sally Cassidy, Reuel
Denney, Jack Getzels, and Michael Maccoby—all colleagues at the University of Chicago; Alexander Morin,
social science editor of the University of Chicago Press;
Howard S. Becker and Warren Peterson, of Community
Studies, Inc., in Kansas City (on whose studies of
school teachers I have heavily relied); John R. Seeley,
of Community Surveys in Indianapolis; Eliot Freidson,
of the City College of New York (on whose study of
student government for the United States National
Student Association I have drawn); Patrick Hazard, of
New Jersey State Teachers College at Trenton; Harold
D. Lasswell; John A. Rice, formerly of Black Mountain
College; Bruce Barton, Jr., education editor of *Time*;
Nathan Glazer; and Evelyn T. Riesman.

I want to express my appreciation to President Fred-
erick Burkhardt of Bennington College for allowing me

[6] The first lecture was published as "The Meandering Procession of American Academia," *Harvard Educational Review*, vol.
26 (1956), pp. 241–262; the second as "Some Observations on
the 'Older' and the 'Newer' Social Sciences," in Leonard D.
White, ed., *The State of the Social Sciences* (Univ. of Chicago
Press, 1956), pp. 319–339; the third as "Teachers Amid Changing
Expectations," *Harvard Educational Review*, vol. 24 (1954), pp.

to draw on these Nebraska lectures for my John Dewey Memorial Lecture at Bennington in June, 1956.[7]

Several foundation grants—some already referred to —have made work on this book possible. One, from the Behavioral Sciences Division of the Ford Foundation, enabled us to set up the Center for the Study of Leisure at the University of Chicago; the concern for cultural diversity which appears in these lectures is one of the Center's major preoccupations. Another, from the Social Science Research Committee of the University of Chicago, aided completion of the manuscript and its typing and preparation for the press by Alice Chandler of the Committee on Human Development.

D.R.

Brattleboro, Vermont
June 1956

106–117—themes further developed in "Thoughts on Teachers and Schools," *Anchor Review*, vol. 1 (1955), pp. 27–60. I am indebted to Professor White and to the editors of the Reviews for permission to draw on these articles in this volume.

[7] See *Some Continuities and Discontinuities in the Education of Women* (Bennington, Vt.: Bennington College, 1957).

PROLOGUE

The plan of these three lectures is to place American higher and secondary school education in its cultural context. In the first, I indicate some of the ways in which the universities serve as models for one another, as academic fashions spread—but I also indicate that there are colleges which are so remote from the leading centers as to be influenced only slowly, if at all, by what happens at the major institutions. I say something also about the ways in which the ferment of innovation and experiment, once so notable a feature of our academic life, now tends to be less yeasty, as on the whole our colleges rise above the evident need for drastic reform. In this connection, I raise the problem of what might be termed "institutional homogenization"—the way in which universities come to resemble large corporations or government agencies, markedly so in seeing public relations as the answer to all dilemmas. And I discuss the related fact that universities today tend to follow national models, and hence are at once less parochial and, arguably, more nationalistic—tied less than before to a provincial sect or municipal culture, but bound all the more firmly to the all-American way.

While the first lecture deals with academic institutions in relation to each other, the second deals with the fields of knowledge (primarily within the social sciences) and their relation to each other. Here the inquiry is somewhat more specialized. I begin with the way in which the social sciences have won a certain freedom, though one still not so secure as that of the natural sciences. I deal with the spread of the movement for interdisciplinary (or integrated, or general education) courses, and with some of the problems presented when men of one discipline encounter in research the men and methods of another. Moreover, I seek to indicate how a discipline tends to become a "veto group" with monopolistic claims—yet, like a monopoly, protecting its adherents and providing certain long-run advantages for research.

The third lecture pays more attention to the customers and constituencies of educators than to movements within the educational world itself. It presents a theory of education as desirably "counter-cyclical," that is, a theory that education should oppose momentary booms and busts in our cultural economy. The application is primarily to the high schools (though references back to the colleges are frequent); the argument runs that progressive education, though it continues to inspire some of the impoverished sectors of American education, becomes less and less truly progressive as most education and much of life has caught up with it. To see this problem in its context involves a description of the community pressures which besiege the public school as compared with those which impinge on the publicly controlled college, and the ways in which the teachers resist such pressures or succumb to them; illustration is drawn from the teaching of social studies. I raise questions as to how students can make contact with excellence when the school program and their own goals are geared to mediocrity.

Thus, I am dealing at times with the spread of ideas, as when I concentrate on the influence in the social sciences of anthropological perspectives, and at times with the spread of educational movements, such as the movement to establish colleges and universities, or the general education movement, or progressivism in the secondary schools. Ideas and movements shade into each other, of course, and the sociology of intellectual life embraces consideration of both; moreover, one can find concepts, such as Trotsky's "law" of uneven and combined development or Harold D. Lasswell's notion on which I shall rely of "restriction through partial incorporation," which can be applied to both.

My coverage of these matters is, however, extremely uneven, resting as it does on quite limited experience: more detailed when I am dealing with the social sciences than with the secondary schools; and no conclusion should be drawn from the resulting bias that there are more innovations under way in the former than in the latter. Moreover, the lectures are more descriptive than programmatic—not because I am a social scientist but because, apart from a few rather general observations on educational strategy, I was not able to muster the innovative wit and committed wisdom a program maker needs.

Following the lectures, a discussion period permitted me to clarify contradictions and to connect themes. In revising the lectures for publication, I have amplified points previously stated too cryptically, often in a footnote, but I have provided bibliographical references only in the rare instances where an article or book was directly relevant. In the main the lectures are presented here in the form in which they were given, with their discursiveness and relatively free association. They stand near the beginning of what, at least for the colleges, we

barely have at present, namely, a sociology of education
—one reason why, despite the dangers of a little knowledge, I allow them to go out into the fixity of print at
this stage.

I

THE ACADEMIC

PROCESSION

ORTHODOXY AND EMANCIPATION IN THE
NINETEENTH-CENTURY COLLEGE

I was reading not long ago, in *Grandmother Brown's Hundred Years*, about the founding of Ohio University at Athens, Ohio, in the 1820s. The New Englanders who had come out there in the first decades of the last century included some who were passionately concerned lest their culture become attenuated in the new setting; they were willing to endure physical but not intellectual or religious poverty. Clergymen ordinarily took the lead in founding academies and colleges, partly to keep the young in the fold and out of secular temptations, and partly to train aspirants for the ministry. Many of the colleges, however, were no sooner founded than the founding fathers were accusing them of deviation from orthodoxy—of Arianism, Unitarianism, godlessness; indeed, such developments often gave rise to new, schismatic colleges which in turn developed their own orthodoxies.[1] As Richard Hofstadter and Walter Metzger have observed in their fine book on the history of academic freedom, these theological controversies anticipate the form, though seldom the content, of later conflicts over academic freedom—both those of the last several generations between business and education and those of today between politics and education. The ministers discovered, as businessmen and legislators were later to do, that by calling something a college, one could hardly help giving it some leeway for self-definition, transcending its partisan or pious origins. The situation resembles that of a parent who wants his son to be mobile socially, to rise to a higher station than his own, while yet fuming at the way he has taken to drink or divorce or voting Republican or whatever else goes in the community with an elevated social-class position.

If this dialectic between the parish and the world is endemic in American education, what has definitely changed is the degree of investment in education as a messianic movement. The struggle both to found and to attend college in the last century sprang often from booster and commercial motives, but there remained in the idea of a college a certain visionary element, whether religious or secularized, which linked education with more than training for professional success—linked it with the promise of a nobler, less demeaning life. Education still has something of this aura in the "underdeveloped" areas of the world, where poor communities

[1] Even fundamentalist sects, suspicious of intellect and opposed to formal theology, have been forced to found their own colleges in order to keep their mobile young within the fold and out of the hands of secularists. (Thomas Le Duc in his interesting study, *Piety and Intellect at Amherst College*, makes clear that in a struggle between piety and learning, one resolution could be for a college to emphasize "character"—a virtue on which classicists and the devout could agree.)

establish colleges as if life itself depended on them, or the glory that makes life worth living.

"Pioneer's Progress"

Any number of autobiographies of distinguished Americans of earlier generations testify to what the struggle for education meant in a day when going to college was something uncommon, and when for a community to possess a college was hardly less a sign of progress than for it to get a railway or canal to wind its way there. For example, Alvin Johnson in *Pioneer's Progress* vividly describes his experience in the 1890s at the then newly founded University of Nebraska: of the classical training he had there which opened up before him what Lionel Trilling, in *The Opposing Self*, eloquently describes as that "other culture" of Greece and Rome. Johnson grew up among the sod huts, but he was no barbarian pioneer, no sabra of the American plain. Likewise, Thorstein Veblen, when he entered Carleton College, was able in some measure to emancipate himself from the constricted world of Norskie farmers and Yankee traders; languages were important to him also as a means of contact with other patterns of culture. For such men, an education meant rescue from a life in a harsh environment—harsh not only physically but emotionally; it was a way out of class and ethnic oppression, a way out of the poverty of horizon in the family, on the farm, and in the small-town community. Of course, we seldom hear from the men who were not stimulated by their college attendance; we know they endured much dreariness and rote learning—but even the trappings of education were then often lent significance by hope and enthusiasm.

We must not forget that, in the nineteenth century and after, many men went to college to roister and so to become gentlemen; Hofstadter and Metzger remind us that before the days of organized sport, the teachers were frequently proctors and patrolmen, barely able to control their charges. Those expelled from college today on disciplinary grounds are a tiny fraction of the minatory discharges of an earlier day—despite panty raids, students are far less rowdy than they used to be. Nevertheless, the creed of the Enlightenment was strong enough to give many educators the sense of participating not so much in a scientific and scholarly as in a missionary movement.

The Failure of Success

Today, as I have indicated, one is not likely to find this spirit inside the U.S.A. One might look for it among some of the depressed Delta Negroes whom the Army taught to read; and here and there—in a remote Idaho valley or Chicago's Back of the Yards or in a small Vermont village—one can find colleges struggling for survival and proud of keeping a beacon alight. But on the whole American higher education is dizzy from success; in spite of all complaints, it is rich, fabulously well attended, and generally taken for granted. Among our sophisticated people, in fact, a great disillusionment has spread.

To be sure, we must not equate the loss of enthusiasm among the professionals in education with the experience of the students themselves, who may appear more sophisticated than they in fact are—and for whom the exploration of self in the college setting can be an ever-renewed source of wonder. As Lyman Bryson has written me, "The most lackadaisical priest may be droning what is heavenly music to someone in the pews and the dullest teacher—even he!—may, by no virtue of his own, be handing out manna to healthy, even if fashionably

disavowed, young appetites." But if we concentrate
now, not on the students, but on the educators, we realize that most of them no longer see their work as an
"Operation Bootstrap" by which a whole society can
be made over, and only a few repeat the early chiliastic
claims for higher education. As a big business in its own
right—whatever its immediate and prospective financial
crises—it can no longer afford the irresponsibility of the
marginal institution. In its relation to the other major
powers in contemporary society, it has experienced what
Harold D. Lasswell terms "restriction by partial incorporation"; that is, the "movement" aspects of higher education have had limits set to their progress by partial
acceptance on the part of what was once the enemy:
the influential Americans who, especially in the post-
Civil War period, worshiped the plainly practical, the
self-made, the ruggedly unscholarly. Today, a modus
vivendi appears in sight between education and business, if not quite yet between education and the politics
of the discontented classes.[2]

Lasswell's concept is perhaps less pessimistic than
Michels' "iron law of oligarchy," which assumes that
every reform movement must become bureaucratized
and hierarchical, or Troeltsch's "law" that every sect
with success becomes a church, bound to repress and
stultify those spontaneous feelings which led to its birth.
For Lasswell assumes that the reform movement does
have an impact, and that it is precisely this which leads
to its becoming incorporated in a new equilibrium at a
higher level. Along this line we can see that education,
whether in the colleges and universities or through the
mass media, has generally moved to liberate Americans

[2] See my essay (written in collaboration with Nathan Glazer),
"The Intellectuals and the Discontented Classes," in Daniel Bell,
ed., The New American Right (New York: Criterion Books,
1955) pp. 56–91.

from regional and parochial attachments; it has been a way of escape from village pressures, whether of gossip or of vigilantism. Indeed, Samuel Stouffer's *Communism, Conformity, and Civil Liberties* shows how decisively college education today introduces people into a "national" culture, so that, for example, Southerners who have graduated from college are closer to college-educated Northerners in their views than to Southerners with a high-school education.[3] But, as a result of the same development, the big universities, which operate on the national scene, lack the protective encapsulation of the parish: they are bigger game, harder to attack but offering more glory to the attacker, than any local college or county weekly ever could be. Thus we face the paradox that higher education in this country is better in general level of performance than it has ever been, yet we hope for less from it as a means of radical cultural renovation.

From Captains to Staff Sergeants of Erudition

In a way, of course, this is true of other aspects of our national prosperity. The businessman who takes a local industry and makes a national combine of it is brother under the skin to the educational reformer who parlays a small denominational college into a national university. But entrepreneurs in business today only crop out along the edges, in marginal companies, or die unsung, their accomplishments buried, in plant or division of a big corporation. And tycoons or reformers are presently found in higher education primarily in small women's colleges or other marginal outposts, or as unsung deans

[3] Cf. my article, "Orbits of Tolerance, Interviewers, and Elites," *Public Opinion Quarterly*, vol. 20 (1956), pp. 49–73; and see also Ernest Havemann and Patricia Salter West, *They Went to College* (New York: Harcourt, Brace and Co., 1952).

in major institutions. Let us remind ourselves that, even a generation ago, there were many exciting figures on the American collegiate scene. Most of us have forgotten the fight Woodrow Wilson waged against the eating clubs of Princeton; we are perhaps more likely to associate Princeton with F. Scott Fitzgerald than with Wilson. How many of us remember Alexander Meiklejohn and his campaigns at Amherst and Wisconsin; Clarence Cook Little and what he tried at Michigan; Arthur E. Morgan and the remaking of Antioch; Glenn Frank's lively Wisconsin; as well as such less embattled captains of erudition as Edmund Ezra Day of Cornell and George Edgar Vincent of Minnesota? The founding of Bennington and Sarah Lawrence and the rise of Reed date from the end of this epoch, and Hutchins at Chicago represented a kind of Indian summer of this rebellious and experimental outlook. (Not believing it could have passed, he blamed the universities themselves as if, had they only a clearer mind and a stronger will, they could have made over the world.) [4]

However, innovation is by no means completely dead; rather, just as big corporations have left innovations to research and development departments and confined

[4] I might add that another kind of Indian summer has been given some of our leading colleges by the attacks of McCarthy and other intellectual commissars. These attacks have come at the time when it could least be said that anything experimental, let alone subversive, was going on at most of these colleges, and when in fact arthritis had often set in, with the wide acceptance among educated people of the fundamental tenets of liberalism. But the attacks, which of course had to be fought, brought exhilaration as well as anxiety and terror to many campuses—much as an elderly man, doubtful of his attractiveness, might reap a certain comfort from a false accusation that he is having an affair with a pretty girl. To be sure, academic heresy and political heresy are not the same thing, but their proponents and opponents are sometimes the same people, and many of the colleges under strong political attack—I think of Sarah Lawrence, Harvard, Antioch, Reed, Chicago—have also been among the most experimental educationally.

the work of their top executive to that of chief public relations officer, so at the big universities what innovation there is seems to have been shifted out of the president's hands into those of the deans. Some of these anonymous men, if more ingratiating than Hutchins or the earlier generations of reformers, have quietly promoted quite far-reaching changes. (It takes modesty and courage in a university president to run interference for a dean more imaginative than he; to be sure, some deans, when things appear quiet, know how to benefit from a lazy or limelight-loving man at the top.) General education at Harvard, humanistic education at MIT, the General College of Minnesota, and a host of smaller and less spectacular notions owe much to the handiwork of such deans. Thus, in a sense, innovation has, in our greatest institutions of learning, become institutionalized and no great revolutionary figure is likely to appear.

THE LOSS OF OBVIOUS MODELS

Summing all this up, it would seem that education in its topmost reaches, and at the secondary school level as much as in the universities, has lost its excitement and enthusiasm for a large part of its professional cadre. As I have already implied, much the same thing has happened to the United States as a whole. We can no longer look abroad for inspiration for our models of cultural and educational advance—nor even react against foreign models which, in so many cases, are busy imitating us. In 1850 Tappan was fighting to make Michigan like Harvard, and in 1900 Gilman was fighting to make Hopkins like Göttingen or Berlin—while Eliot was fighting against the German model, to make Harvard an American university, indigenously relevant (Ernest Earnest gives a lively account of all this in *Academic Procession*). But in 1950? Europeans and Japanese, West Africans and Burmese, now come here to look for models or invite American professors to visit and bring with them the "American Way" in higher education. This is understandable, for at least at the graduate level, our universities—and many, many more of them than simply Harvard, Columbia, Chicago—are in their energy and accomplishments as good as any the planet offers.

As I have remarked, this stalemate of success has overtaken many other aspects of our national life. Save in the South, we are not an underdeveloped country any more (and the South, of course, is rapidly being jerked out of colonialism). Whereas a generation ago American expatriates who went to Europe were quicker to seize on what was avant-garde there than most Europeans themselves, complacent as the latter could often be about their cultural superiority, today the American in Paris or Rome can wryly observe the spread of American fashions in design, fiction, music, and film. The time for maturation of an idea or a style which is possible for creative workers in an outpost or a marginal group is not easily available to those in the centers from which diffusion occurs; and, in part because higher education has made such spectacular advances in this country, diffusion of our cultural models occurs with unprecedented speed. Like a mobile man who has shot to the top so fast as to arrive there with undissipated energies and time to look around, American intellectual and educational leadership often seems haunted by the question where to go from here.

Search for a Scale of Judgment

Of course the problem of where to go next which besets the richest and most advanced institutions, a problem they often manage to postpone by keeping an eye mainly on each other, as do the Big Three in the design of automobiles, does not beset those schools whose goal can simply be to overtake the leaders. But in education it is perhaps not as easy as in manufacturing to say who is the leader, who is at the top, or which way is up: there is no World Series or All-American team. Harvard once assumed that it could call to its faculty anyone from anywhere in the country, but this is no longer quite so. Along with all the "nationalizing" tendencies mentioned a moment ago has come a growth of complexity so that no single prestige system can dominate the great variety of subsystems, any more than the first families of one city can dominate the whole country. The president of a land-grant college is not likely to feel that any Ivy League college is really relevant for his problems, which include how to get his institution's name changed from Morrill State College to Morrill State University while not losing his agricultural economists or professors of forestry.

To be sure, there has been one very interesting effort to rank institutions by other than the plainly irrelevant criteria of size or endowment or age, and that is by the series of studies carried out at Connecticut Wesleyan of the collegiate origins of American scholars. In their volume on *The Younger American Scholar: His Collegiate Origins,* Knapp and Greenbaum rank colleges in terms of their proportionate production of recognized scholars. Most of those at the top are small liberal arts colleges such as Reed, Swarthmore, Oberlin, Carleton, Chicago, and Antioch. Yet I wonder how many administrators have pondered this list with an eye to improving their home institutions, or how many faculties could accurately guess the leaders in this league! And of course students are even less likely to know these batting averages, though eventually the news does get around.[5] Thus, the flow of influence, from institutions which serve as models to others in academia, is one not easily marked out, and one cannot say that there is a single recognizable system of prestige. College public relations departments seldom vaunt curricular developments, unless they can be claimed as unique, but rather such more easily demonstrable matters as new buildings and equipment, numbers of students, and alumni gifts.

THE SNAKE-LIKE PROCESSION

Despite these difficulties, I am going to present a concededly oversimplified picture in order to try to capture certain large trends in the movement and rhythm of American academic development. It may be illuminating to see the avant-garde, both educational and more generally cultural, as the head of a snake-like procession— the head of which is often turning back upon itself, as at present, while the middle part seeks to catch up with where the head once was. When the middle part becomes aware, as doesn't always happen, that the position of the head has shifted, it may try to turn in two directions at once.

We might begin by asking in what direction is such a university as that of Nebraska turning, i.e., what are the models to which it and others like it look for possible direction? There is no doubt that colleges and universities in this country do model themselves upon each other, and the question remains: which other? All one

[5] It seems possible that the news spreads a good deal faster today than it once did, thanks in part to more energetic recruitment by the colleges and more energetic guidance by high school counselors. The rate of change in fashion has accelerated in this as in so many other areas. Witness the boom in applications for Oberlin, Reed, Radcliffe, Swarthmore.

has to do is read catalogues to realize the extent of this isomorphism. Once one enters, let us say, the state university league, this involves the full line of departments. People who come into the league to teach, having done graduate work elsewhere, bring with them an image of what a proper university should look like—and this image consists truly of castles in the air, not located on a particular, carefully studied terrain. The image may have been formed in England or Germany, in Berkeley or Cal Tech, in Chicago or Columbia or Michigan or the University of Iowa. But of course, it need not have so specific a location: isomorphism in this area as in others depends not only on direct imitation but on general social patterns which are refracted in specific institutional forms. The tendency to add rather than to integrate is, according to John Kouwenhoven, a peculiarily American one; he observes it in city and rural-section layout, skyscraper architecture, jazz improvisation, the assembly line, comic strips, and so on.[6] The one or two thousand courses given in a large college or university likewise reflect this willingness to add, this omnipresent university extension. Moreover, as my colleague Richard J. Storr has pointed out to me, to bring a few professors from one place and to set them up in business in another is a relatively inexpensive operation (notably so in the humanities); to add a new department often costs less than to add a new dormitory or a hockey rink.

"Locals" versus "Cosmopolitans"

Such a new department, then, oriented to the places where its members were trained, may try to set new sights for the university to which it has been moved. But understandably, these new outsiders or "cosmo-

[6] See "What's American about America?", *Colorado Quarterly*, vol. 3, Winter 1955.

politans"[7] do not always have an easy time of it. The drive which brought them there may have spent itself in that very act, and the home-guard, the "locals," of the university may resent and frustrate any efforts at further departure from its locally approved ways. It is a rare institution where some departments do not carefully staff themselves with home-brew talent and thus avoid disagreeable comparisons; the locals or "nativists" will insist complacently that what is done at Harvard or Oxford, Ann Arbor or Princeton, is quite meaningless in Fayetteville, Lincoln, Parkville, Missouri, or at Doane College or Peru State Teachers. Home-brew is easier to take in some flavors than in others: if one wants a good physics department, it will hardly do, but in agronomy or English one could make a go of it. At the University of Illinois, as I understand it, the home-guard was able to defeat itinerants from so near a place as Iowa State College—economists who had the bad luck not to have done their graduate work at Urbana.

The Home Guard as a "Front," Facing Both Ways

The home guard is, by its nature, likely to be integrated into the local community; its members play golf with the local realtors, car dealers, and doctors in the small towns, and are active in civic associations in the larger ones. Where they are intellectual fellow-travelers of the cosmopolitans, they can help integrate them also into the community, or at least defend them against local pressure; where they are not, they can be extremely effective antagonists of the cosmopolitans by "explain-

[7] Sociologists will recognize here Robert K. Merton's distinction between locals and cosmopolitans in his article, "Patterns of Influence: A Study of Interpersonal Influence and of Communications Behavior in a Local Community," in Paul F. Lazarsfeld and Frank Stanton, eds., *Communications Research 1948–1949* (New York: Harper & Bros., 1949), pp. 180–219.

ing" locally just how bad, how radical, they are—a reaction which, in times of general fear of radicalism,
has helped to erode academic freedom at a number of
institutions. Moreover, the home-guarders are typically
concerned with the university's service functions to students and to the locale, rather than with research and
with participation in the national intellectual life; they
have no objection to growth, much as this may lead to
departure from tradition, if it involves larger numbers of
students, more popular courses, and athletic prowess,
whereas the itinerant cosmopolitans bring with them, as
already implied, a more elitist conception of academia
which emphasizes a small but select student body and
a research-oriented curriculum, and deprecates athletics.
(Naturally, as with all such typologies, there are individuals who fit neither category, or combine elements
from both.)

Veblen saw the university president as the very
archetype of home-guarder, so mixed in with the local
business community as to be indistinguishable from it,
save in possessing the promotional gifts of a Captain of
Erudition. In my own observation, and that of other
present-day observers, the president is as likely to be
fighting home-guardism, with elements in his faculty—
and especially perhaps in the lower administration, including many department heads—sitting tight. Yet if he
alienates the home guard too much, he will have only
the cosmopolitans to fall back upon—mobile men who
will in many cases be moving up and out; they cannot
help him much with the legislature or the local Legion
post or the Grange.[8]

---

[8] The president seems secure in his job at colleges located in
the very head of the procession, where he is protected by traditions of civility and of faculty democracy, and in the lower
reaches, where he protects himself by autocratic control—in the

The president has less chance to move (rarely can he move back to his old league, into a professorship), and he can certainly not count on moving; whatever mobility drive he has must go into the institution itself. And here is where the prestige of other institutions is apt to be used as a debating point for adding new fields and departments and new men from elsewhere to staff them. "If Chicago has a sociology department, why can't we have one?"—this must have been asked for several generations, as this new field spread throughout the country until only in the Ivy League do there remain significant colleges, such as Hopkins or Wesleyan, which take a certain wry pride in resisting this newcomer among the disciplines. And our medical schools have been under the same kind of scrutiny and pressure. "How can you call yourselves a medical school without a pathologist?"—the Flexnerites asked such questions in eliminating virtually all the Class C medical schools. Medical schools of course have been "nationalized" as colleges have not and many among the latter neither die nor rise but hang grimly on because someone sometime gave them a plant, a president, and a push. But I am not talking now, as I briefly shall later, about those institutions so far below the level of current discourse as not to be faced with pressures for improvement, but about those near enough the top in one league or another to be influenced. And as I have indicated, this influence leads to a tug of war between the home-guard locals who make a fortress of local traditions, no matter how happenstance these are, and the cosmopolitan itinerants who bring the prestige of other institutions, often without making too much of an effort to adapt their models to the local potentialities.

---

middle he is vulnerable much in the way a union leader often is, and must bring home the bacon from the legislature or rich alumni to prevent replacement by a more aggressive leader.

Regional versus National Models

Let me illustrate this characteristic conflict by reference to the experience I had when I went as a young graduate of Harvard Law School to teach at the University of Buffalo Law School. At least half the faculty and all but one of its younger men were Harvard trained, for at that time Harvard dominated legal education, the world of the nationally oriented law schools, as no university now dominates legal, medical, or graduate education. Most of these Harvard-trained people wanted to teach those courses which, as students, they had learned were the subjects of greatest intellectual excitement—and these were then mainly oriented around the federal government, including such topics as labor law, constitutional law, administrative law, and so on. (Moreover, the contacts of these Harvard cosmopolitans were in Washington, and they could try to place their best students there.) As against this, several faculty members thought Buffalo should develop a curriculum that was not merely a minor league (though excellent) version of the Eastern Seaboard schools but rather one which was designed with reference to the particular problems of Western New York. But such a change—to a more region-oriented outlook—would have been defined as an intellectual defeat, as having become provincial under the impact of local pressures, as a discredited vocationalism concerned with the State bar exams and the local job market. For a variety of reasons, the experiment was never made. In any event, as it turned out, the good students were in only a few cases interested in preparing themselves for careers confined to Upper New York State; for most of them, their models were their itinerant teachers and their eyes were on what the Supreme Court was up to, or the S.E.C., and not on Buffalo's City Planning Commission or Erie County's school consolidation program. In contrast, the home-guard faculty had on the whole little to offer in the way of a vision of a specialized but distinguished small school; they were apt to recall how it had been in their day, but failed to see (as Everett Hughes likes to put it) in what ways an institution has to change in order to remain the same.

Identification with Trends, with Science, or with Siwash

In this example we can glimpse another factor at work in academic isomorphism. If we assume that there is such a thing as a true scholar, he would not be swayed by trends (or even by the countering of trends)—by discovering that students had their eye on Washington, or that the Supreme Court got more headlines than the municipal bench; each would be relevant for him, not in terms of professional or student fashion—that is, in terms of power, but in terms of its intrinsic significance in his own transcending preoccupations. I think we have all met such men, in medieval history or the classics, for instance, who profess utter unconcern with the current market quotation on their disciplines and are even prepared to see them sink lower on the national exchange. Some, understandably enough, wring a small "secondary gain" from their position by means of a Pharisaical pride vis-à-vis more worldly colleagues, especially social scientists. But most professors are not so independent of general cultural values and imperatives. As already mentioned, Veblen argued, as did Upton Sinclair, that scholars were subverted by businessmen in the guise of administrators; but I think most of us would today grant that professors are themselves apt to apply business standards to their work—just as I think it also to be the case that businessmen have increasingly adopted non-commercial values as they have become more sophisticated. More precisely, we academic people tend to judge ourselves as would a firm: does our university offer a full line; is it properly diversified; what is our Dun and Bradstreet rating in the proper accreditation association; how many students do we have, in absolute numbers and relative to those colleagues who, in sociological lingo, comprise our reference group? In fact, a state university, living on biennial appropriations, needs a very pertinacious president to do any long-term planning. Whereas Veblen thought professors ought to despise and reject administrators as displaced businessmen who should be sent back to their predatory trades, it may be that professors today look down on deans and college presidents for different reasons, and with some envy, because they think: "There but for the grace of non-promotion go I."

In the course of my work on behalf of the inquiry into teachers' apprehensions, I had occasion to talk to a number of college professors concerning academic freedom; and I was struck by the extent to which many identified themselves with their colleges rather than with their subject-matter or with the professoriate as a whole. This often led them, not to criticize "their" institution for poor behavior in some *cause célèbre* or quiet firing, but rather to explain and apologize: they would say, "Sure, our President let So-and-so go after the Velde Committee got after him, but you must realize that he has to go before the legislature for a new medical research building this year; and anyway, So-and-so handled himself ineptly and was, for a state school like this, most indiscreet. . . ." Indeed, this tendency to turn on the victim and criticize him—and doubtless most victims in cases of academic freedom are tactless, or disingenuous, or too ingenuous—would seem to be part of the same public relations orientation in which the faculty understands the plight of the administration almost too well. Men who would not inhibit their frankness of speaking out for the sake of their own careers or peace of mind are often willing to do so for the sake of their college, lest they embarrass it in its relation to parents, alumni, the community, or other relevant constituencies outside the world of scholarship. There is in this a selfless and in many ways admirable loyalty to the institution and to the group of colleagues who momentarily compose it. And the professors who do this are not only the home guard who have few wider loyalties anyhow but the cosmopolitans who also try to maintain their loyalty to science. Understandably, the professors, in return for identifying themselves with the college and even on occasion sacrificing for it their wider identity with the cosmos of scholarship, require of their institution that it rate, that people know of it and think well of it.

Thus, a good deal of academic expansion and isomorphism is the result of administrators responding not only to their own drives but to those of their faculties, though the latter put the onus on the administrators and blame them for carrying out their half-secret wishes. What on the student and alumni level may take the form of wanting a winning football team, at the very least in order to explain one's choice of college to one's gang, may on the professional level appear in a comparable assumption. The assumption is that every decent university will offer courses in archaeology, in Tudor history, or in the sociology of small groups, whether or not there exist topflight people to fill these lines, and even if to get them filled means sacrificing the possibility of building up a uniquely exhilarating department out of offerings not currently regarded as among the blue chips of academia.

The Mobile Middle of the Procession

Now there is no doubt that this process, this dialectic

between parochial and cosmopolitan models, has re-
sulted in giving the snake-like procession a great deal of
momentum at its middle levels. Take, for example, what
seems to have happened at a border state university
during the regime of a politician-president who cared
mightily for good football teams and, according to report, not a whit for scholarly distinction. It seems that
strong department chairmen could go to him and say,
"Look, Columbia has a good man in colonial history; I
believe we should . . ."—and the president would happily agree, nothing was too good for his school (much
as nothing was too good—for example, the first-rate
Southern Review—for Huey Long's pet Louisiana State
University). These professors knew that, should they
get into the papers, they would not be protected by the
administration; but as long as things were quiet, the
president would back them with money and enthusiasm.
The shrewd men of his faculty, in other words, treated
him much as Victorian wives eager for culture treated
their tycoon spouses: the wives conspired with each
other to drag their men to the opera, to tap them for
the symphony, and otherwise to play on their desire to
be well thought of in the new domains their money
opened up to them. It is in part such phenomena that
I have in mind when I say that, if professors have fallen
prey to business values, so businessmen and some politicians have likewise been infiltrated by academic values.

How to Handle Trustees

Indeed, so much is the latter the case that many university administrators are mistaken in supposing that
their businessmen trustees want what they pretend often to want, namely a "businesslike" administration of
the university. Some of them would not have become
trustees if they wanted a life composed of entirely homo-

geneous activities and evaluations; they may express a belief in such a life—a life free of contradictions and tensions—but their actions belie them. Especially the more complex and sophisticated businessmen would not appreciate a world populated wholly by people like themselves; it would not be interesting; they want their minister, their physician, their university president (and on occasion their personnel director) to tell them that they are miserable materialistic sinners, and make them pay for the privilege, and for their privileges. I recall once attending a luncheon of the Citizens Board of the University of Chicago. The Board was then composed of Chicago businessmen who might someday, if they behaved themselves, graduate into becoming trustees; most of them, however, had not had much cultivation as potential buttresses for academic freedom and vitality. At the table where I sat, rather reactionary talk flowed, led by a red-faced public relations executive who thought the University was badly managed, had too many Communists, and all the rest of it. Then Mr. Hutchins got up to talk. His first words were that he had two regrets as he looked forward to surrendering his stewardship of the University: first, that there wasn't enough red in the University budget; and, second, that there weren't enough Reds on the faculty! He went on in that vein, and when he ended was cheered to the echo, and by no one more than my tablemate who couldn't say enough about what a wonderful man Hutchins was. Magnetic leadership, such as Hutchins had, can get away with more than usually appears on the surface; one of the things it discovers, by taking chances, is that we do not always unequivocally want what we say we want. Or, to put it another way, we have wants of which, amid the noise and rhetoric of our talk, we are unaware, until someone comes along with the courage to brush aside our manifest claims and desires. And certainly when we consider the

relations between Harper of Chicago and the elder
Rockefeller, or Andrew White and Ezra Cornell, or Gilman and the trustees of Johns Hopkins' estate, we can
see that many businessmen, who may fear to think
themselves sentimental, can be grateful when someone
gives them a good hard-headed reason to do something
decent and unconventional.[9]

TURNS AND TWISTS AT THE HEAD OF THE PROCESSION

The Highbrow-Lowbrow Alliance

Hutchins assumed in these remarks that the way for a
university to advance was by attaining financial and intellectual irreverence and exuberance (the latter mistak-
enly, or perhaps only paradoxically and in order to
shock, linked to the Communists and thus falling in
with their own image of themselves as true rebels).
However, this is a mood rather than a program, and the
programs that have emanated from leading institutions
in recent years have been of a less spectacular sort. They
include a renewed emphasis on undergraduate teach-

[9] On several occasions when I have happened to see professors
in conference together with trustees, I have noticed a tendency
for the former to appear worldly-wise, practical, and even cynical,
whereas the trustees have been the high-minded and "academic"
ones. Likewise, when the Bell Telephone Company set up its
remarkable program in humanistic education at the University
of Pennsylvania—a program which required a small number of
middle-level phone executives drawn from all parts of the country
to spend a year in a liberal arts curriculum (including James Joyce,
Bartok, Mies van der Rohe, Lewis Mumford, et al.), it was hard
for some of the professors who addressed the group to believe
there was no need for an immediate vocational pay-off and that
they could be as highbrow as they knew how to be; the Telephone executives who set the program up had to emphasize many
times that they were not looking for industrial-relations gimmicks.
I know that such encounters are not typical of trustee-faculty

ing, on interdisciplinary courses and general education, including a spate of programs in American civilization, a revived interest in the humanities, in theology and in values generally. The avant-garde has added other pre-occupations. For example, at some Ivy League schools and at Chicago, there has developed a strong highbrow fondness for lowbrow or popular culture, and a knowl-edge of comic strips, jazz, baseball, Westerns, and soap opera is occasionally *de rigueur* if one is to be up to date. In some quarters, this is part of a kind of late love affair with the United States, accompanied by a rejec-tion of Europe (witness some of the contributions, in-cluding my own, to the *Partisan Review* symposium on "America and the Intellectuals"). Likewise, much of the so-called "New Conservatism" has developed as an avant-garde rejection of middlebrow liberalism—there would be no fun in being a new conservative if all one's colleagues shared the views of Senator Bricker or the late Senator Wherry.

In fact, the shifts of opinion that go on among the avant-garde, even when these include a belief in a closer

---

relations throughout the length of the academic procession, but I also know that higher education, like other cultural institutions, no longer is regarded as an affair only for culture-hungry women and for men, such as ministers and teachers, who are widely viewed as not quite manly.

Where trustees and regents are less enlightened than at a few leading institutions, I have sometimes speculated concerning the job-description of an appropriate university president. I have said that he should preferably be a man so arrogant and unapproach-able that no parent, unacculturated trustee, or potential donor could possibly tell him what might be termed an off-color ac-ademic freedom story of the type: "Wouldn't it be a good idea, Jim, if our friend, Professor Contrarius, were not to be given that raise—might take the hint and go somewhere else, huh?" Perhaps he could even be a little bit stuffy, so that no one could dream of regaling him with an off-color story of any sort, let alone calling him by his first name. After a bit of casting about the American scene, it occurred to me that some haughty but charming Englishman would perhaps best fit my job-description.

attention to the American scene, are quite generally
based on a desire to put oneself at a distance from the
world of the academic middlebrow. Usually, this is the
only part of the procession of American academia of
which the intellectual leaders at the head are aware, for
it is easy to forget the enormous contrasts that can still
be found among people all of whom bear the title "Professor."

The Stragglers in the Procession

There are plenty of colleges where the professors read
nothing heavier than *Life* or the *Saturday Evening
Post* or the local paper. The avant-garde, in looking back
at the middle ranks of the procession, has ordinarily no
idea how far these have traveled away from the bottom
ranks: we see here a general phenomenon of hierarchy,
that to the rich the poor may look more alike than they
do to themselves, and to the poor, the rich. By the same
token, the head of the procession cannot "see" the tail
end, because the middle obscures its view, and the tail
end moves so far behind the avant-garde turns and
twists that it ordinarily fails to learn, for instance, that
liberalism is out of date, or anti-clericalism, at many
leading places.[10]

The Academic Tastemakers

But the middlebrow is not similarly defended against
shifts in highbrow fashions of thought. He will often
have staked a great deal of his drive and hope on imi-

[10] This statement has to be qualified in the light of the many
short-circuits in our politics and culture which diffuse avant-garde
developments to all but the most deprived—precisely through
such post-Chatauqua agencies as *Life*, the *Post*, CBS, and some
big-budget movies.

tating at his college some plank in a program developed at one of the pace-setters for his league. For him
to learn that the pace-setter has changed course may
completely dishearten him. Let me illustrate what I have
in mind by reference to a conversation with a group of
indisputably highbrow professors at Columbia. I was
speaking of my visit several years ago to the University of
Arkansas, where I had never been before, and of how
much I admired the work being done there in the arts
and theatre, and especially the modern theatre. The
work, I remarked, seemed to me less outstanding than
that at wealthier state universities like Wisconsin or Illinois, but it was pleasant to see boys from the Arkansas
Ozarks doing modern dance. My friends interrupted to
say how awful they thought this was; one of them
quoted Santayana or someone to the effect that football
was America's great contribution to the ballet, and said
it would be better if the boys weren't corrupted by their
University's efforts at uplift. I was grateful that no Arkansas professor or state legislator who had struggled to
bring high culture to Fayetteville was there to hear this.

The Appeal of Heresy

I trust that in these remarks, which aim to be descriptive, I am not patronizing either Arkansas or Columbia.
At both places, many of the more alert faculty members are looking for a way up in the intellectual world,
but at each the trail markers point in different directions. At both, the professors and administrators pride
themselves on being ahead of the game, on being for-
ward-looking—even if among some it is now forward
to look backward. And unquestionably culture advances, and so does education, as the result of such not
entirely saintly motives; many of us need to feel we are
being a bit heretical, a bit out of step. We look askance,

and with some reason, at the TV comic who feels he is going great if his Hooper rating holds up, while we look with more sympathy on the author who wonders if he is slipping because the Book-of-the-Month Club took his last novel (even if there is evidence that the BOMC is rising).

Erich Fromm has suggested to me that our need to feel heretical is perhaps stronger when we have made compromises in other aspects of our lives (though in some instances having made a compromise leads to a rigid need to defend compromise as such), so that what I am saying now is only superficially contradictory to the point made earlier about the business and public relations values shared by many academic people. That is, we need aspects of heresy in order to reassure ourselves that we have not sold out, that we have not become mere conformists. We might even view this, by extension, as a kind of "countervailing power" (in Kenneth Galbraith's phrase) inside the individual, reflecting the division of values in the academic and the general culture.

Such tendencies must be one factor in a phenomenon which turned up in the Teacher Apprehension Study; Paul F. Lazarsfeld found that, at many avant-garde and middle-level institutions, the respondents described themselves as not only more liberal than the administration, the alumni, and the community wherein the college is located, but also as more liberal than each other, so that almost everybody is more liberal than everybody else. To some extent this reflects the fact that in a period of political reaction people may declare themselves as slightly less left than they feel, while assuming that everyone else is more candid than they, thus coming to think themselves more isolated among colleagues than would be warranted if what sociologists term their "pluralistic ignorance" could be dissipated. To some extent, this finding, as Professor Lazarsfeld has pointed out, also reflects the fact that the truly more liberal professors at the leading institutions are generally the more active-minded and productive ones, and thus set the tone to which the others seek to conform. Moreover, just as in a suburb or housing project of marginal status or in a mental hospital one can find people who will tell the interviewer that *they* don't really belong there and will soon move on, so in a college community many professors understandably want to think of themselves as different from the rest, thus having a motive to misperceive actual similarities. Indeed, in visiting colleges in the summer of 1955 in connection with this study, Mark Benney and I talked to quite a few crusty self-styled reactionaries on liberal campuses who enjoyed their roles as rebels but would hardly qualify as stalwarts for reaction in one of the more benighted colleges.

To readers who are not academic people, it may perhaps come as a dismaying discovery that professors, like other people, engage in marginal differentiation and sometimes overrate the importance of distinctions which, to the outsider, seem negligible. In part, I would argue that the outsider often blurs differences which really do matter in the life of the mind and eventually, I would hope, in the life of the body politic. But even when the differences are less than vital, knowledge does advance when professors act as sounding boards for each other and critics for each other; in this way a great many positions are differentiated and new combinations sometimes found. Scholarship, like other human activities, proceeds through the mixed motives of its devotees, and the professorial desire to be different (though, as we have seen, not different enough) is one source of the critical temper; indeed, an enormous amount of work goes on, which often leads to new findings, simply to prove that some other professor is wrong or crazy or has missed something. Freedom of speech and of investigation would, I fear, soon die out if they could only be claimed by the pure in heart, though I also fear that in many important areas they are dying because we lack the saving remnant of a few who are pure in heart.

Everett Hughes likes to point out that no college can exist solely for students seeking enlightenment, without also catering to students seeking marriage, useful contacts, or four more years on the old man's payroll. More generally, minority intellectual activities could hardly exist without harnessing against the general majority culture some of the same motives, such as fear to be alone, malice, or the wish for prestige, which along with sunnier and nobler drives support the culture. If this is not understood, people, including academicians, will despise academicians too readily for not in general being more heroic than they are. In fact, once one leaves the intellectual avant-garde and ventures into the middle range of colleges which have suffered much from public attack during the years of the Cold War, one can find (as the Teacher Apprehension Study did) a heartening number of defiant men who are at once apprehensive and unbowed; and there are such men holding exposed positions in the avant-garde too.

The Ambiguities of Excellence

My concern in this lecture is, however, more with colleges as models for each other than with men as models for each other. I have no very clear idea as to how many pace-setter or avant-garde institutions there are which today influence wide collegiate orbits. A generation ago, as I remarked earlier, there were centers of ferment both in the Ivy League and in some of the big state universities like Wisconsin and Minnesota, as well as in some small liberal arts colleges throughout the country. At present there are undoubtedly a great many more places where some school or department is in the forefront of research, even though the major training of research men is still done at a handful of major universities.[11] There has been in general a tremendous advance in the level of instruction for what I would guess to be the first third of the academic procession. Undergraduates are now given books to read which professors a generation ago often had not read, or would have considered too difficult; and not only has there been a movement away from textbooks but the textbooks themselves have gotten on the whole much better.[12]

So far has this development gone at a few avant-garde places that I have had to consider the paradoxical possibility that teachers can be too erudite for the full de-

[11] In an unpublished paper, "Developments in the Behavioral Sciences during the Past 20 Years," Bernard Berelson shows that the men who have made important contributions to the social sciences, as judged by their colleagues, were trained principally, and now are connected with, what he calls "the Big Five": Harvard, Chicago, Columbia, Yale, California. The same paper, however, indicates a certain provincialism in the selection of contributions (very few European scholars are within the purview of the judges, for instance), thus supporting my argument later in these lectures (pp. 101–107, *infra*) on the new nationalism of American scholarship.

[12] It is fascinating, in the leaflets put out by textbook publishers giving the names of colleges that have adopted a particular book, to trace the spread of highbrow thinking into the academic hinterland: there are many books which are in use virtually throughout the snake-like procession. To be sure, some of these books have, like Shakespeare, something for everybody; others, of course, are read in different places with very different understandings and overtones; still others may represent a young instructor's effort to deny the facts of local limitation (it often takes such a person several years to learn the local customs and taboos). Many publishers take very seriously their responsibility for the level of higher education (while others refuse books that will not sell in carload lots); and their agents on the road—like the detail men of the drug houses—bring the news of new academic formulae to the isolated and the unenterprising.

velopment of their students: the latter are easily led to feel that there is little left for them to discover. When I was in college, we considered—to take an instance— most of our English and modern language professors as rather stuffy if learned worthies, who had read or liked nothing more recent than Thackeray or possibly Thomas Hardy. Joyce, T. S. Eliot, Proust were hardly mentioned, let alone American writers of any sort—Melville, perhaps, but not Faulkner, Gertrude Stein, Glenway Wescott, Dos Passos or Ring Lardner. This left the initiative to the students, and certainly many of us did not seize it and remained in ignorance of much that is valuable; but for others professorial pedantry and somnolence were countered by student vitality. Today, of course, Joyce, Eliot, Kafka, Proust, Faulkner are standard fare in many humanities programs—occasionally even in the better secondary schools. To be sure, as Lionel Trilling points out in *Freud and the Crisis of Our Culture*, these writers are still avant-garde; no new, greatly creative movement has replaced them as rallying points. Moreover, some professors of English, like Trilling or Leslie Fiedler, today write novels and stories themselves and show that they are not only scholars but lively and worldly men; in addition, these men read the *Kenyon Review*, the *Hudson Review*, the *Partisan Review*, the *Sewanee Review*, the *Pacific Spectator*, and all the rest, sometimes even write and edit them. Thus, the students readily learn that there is hardly any room left in which they can outflank their teachers and win the feeling of independence which comes in this way. Some of what appears as conformism among the young may be due to this.

But that the students so readily conclude this is also a result of their conformity, else they might be less impressed by the learning of their teachers and more aware of the latter's lack of concern with personal growth for themselves and for students. A teacher devoted at once to his subject and to his students' growth through that subject will not inhibit independence no matter how wide and up-to-date his knowledge. The very concept of the avant-garde may lead us astray here, for while education to be meaningful must make contact with the contemporary concerns students have, it must also communicate freshness of perception, new ways of seeing, rather than mere novelty of method or topic. It is thus not the truly creative teachers who tend to turn their students into somewhat apathetic, unadventurous captives but rather the academic gamesmen whom our graduate schools of arts and sciences tend to select and foster, at least in the humanities and the social sciences.

This tends to happen, I am suggesting, in our graduate schools and in the more high-power colleges which are dominated by overshadowing graduate schools. But I have very little idea how widespread this phenomenon is. Certainly it is not at all frequent in comparison with the many institutions where the students are still ahead of the faculty, and out of boredom or impatience are occasionally venturesome.

MOVEMENT IN THE MIDDLE RANKS

Many colleges which twenty years ago were in the trough of complacency have been redecorated, as it were. This includes, I would suppose, some of the already famous like Yale, Brown, and Pennsylvania, and some of the less well known like Wooster and the University of Kansas. Hardly any of the state universities has been without some major effort in the liberal arts, and no part of the country is exempt. It is thus my over-all judgment that the differences which once separated the distinguished from the run-of-the-mill institutions have been greatly reduced. And this is one reason why the salience of the centers of decisive influence (I am speaking now of the undergraduate, not the graduate, level) has also been reduced: rather than having a few experimental pioneers, we have now something on the order of a hundred quite good schools moving along at fairly fast clip in pursuit of the ever-turning head of the procession.

So far, I have spoken as if the colleges in the middle ranks, those not quite in the avant-garde, looked only toward the front, either to where the avant-garde once was and is still thought to be, or occasionally, through the short circuits of mass communication, to where it is now. But not all these colleges, let alone all the faculties in them, are on the move, or keep their eyes focused toward the front. Some are focused on where they have just come from, or on the tail end of the procession, and they are so impressed with how far they have come that they do not try to go further. As we have already seen, many teachers colleges and small denominational schools are engaged in upgrading themselves into liberal arts colleges or universities. When this happens, some of the faculty may hark back to earlier, more limited aims, while others, brought in as part of the upgrading process, may think in terms of the liberal arts orbits in which they have themselves been trained. In some denominational schools, this transition might be symbolized in forms of conflict long since outdated among the middle and upper ranks of academia: thus, an argument over social dancing or over the teaching of evolution might represent an effort of the traditional constituency of a church-dominated college to call a halt to change.

When social scientists at such colleges were interviewed in the Teacher Apprehension Study, they were frequently ignorant of *causes célèbres* of academic freedom that were staple conversational topics at avant-garde institutions; they did not follow civil-liberties cases on the national scene—or, indeed, much of anything on the national scene—even though a few of the older men might belong to the American Association of University Professors. The visitor would occasionally be told at such places: "We've all the academic freedom we want here"—a pretty sure sign that they could not have had the faintest notion of what academic freedom embraces, save perhaps that it is something college professors are supposed to possess and therefore something that they, as bearers of that estate, ought to respond to.

Problems of the Catholic Colleges

Although Catholic colleges were of course included in the sample of this Study, I was unable to visit more than a handful, and I know much less about the range of Catholic institutions than about the Protestant-controlled schools (and as to the latter, I don't feel cognizant of all the many variations either). In talking with several thoughtful priests concerning the survey, I found them understandably concerned to know how the Catholic colleges compared with the Protestant and the secular ones—matters as to which Paul F. Lazarsfeld's and Wagner Thielens' forthcoming *The Academic Man in a Time of Crisis* will contain some fascinating indications; in general, it seems fair to say that the major Catholic universities move in much the same intellectual world as their secular counterparts, while the small Catholic colleges, like their small Protestant counterparts (and like many of the teachers colleges), move in the great majority of cases in a very different, more traditional world.

Yet the Catholics, as late-comers to America, have not been able, even where they might have so desired, to maintain a system of higher education unaffected by

Protestant norms; indeed (as I have learned from Everett Hughes and from the work of such Catholic sociologists as Father Joseph Fichter), Protestant models have influenced in subtle ways even liturgical behavior and parish organization. Nevertheless, in part as a reaction to such influences, there are tendencies among Catholic educators—stronger, of course, in some regions and some teaching orders than in others—to try to develop a total educational plant which is self-contained and sealed off from Protestant models, whether these are looked to in terms of excellence alone or also in terms of interfaith public relations. Thus, in the Teacher Apprehension Study one could find Catholic professors whose identifications were with the Church or their order or even diocese rather than with their intellectual discipline or with the academic fraternity at large. Such men would occasionally express satisfaction that proponents of "intemperate" academic freedom, of "license," were now on the defensive and that teachers were becoming more cautious and "responsible." As already indicated, such comments were more likely to be made by respondents at the smaller Catholic colleges, whereas at the large universities one would find much the usual smörgåsbord of courses and of viewpoints—sometimes imported by laymen (by no means always Catholic) teaching architecture or economic theory or physical chemistry.

Isomorphism combined with autarchy means that there will eventually be priest accountants and Notre Dame-trained physicists, but during the transition the full complement will be maintained by allowing teachers to come in who are not trained in ethics and dogmatics. In a way, as one Catholic lay teacher informed me, this policy is safer for the Catholic schools than for their fundamentalist Protestant counterparts, for in the former one can count on students who have usually had a parochial high school education and a faculty most of whom are true believers, while in the Protestant school one must fight a constant battle for orthodoxy and hence can less afford a deviant faculty member. (He did not add, as I would have, that Protestant fundamentalism can be far more dogmatic than the Pope.) It is also true that the cleric, by virtue of his robe, has a certain protection in matters outside his faith—though of course what is "outside" is always open to question and redefinition; in the field of economics, for example, a liberal priest can stand on the Papal Encyclicals against a business community that demands obedience to its credo of free enterprise.

In similar fashion, the Catholic colleges have often held out for a version of liberal education—that is, an emphasis on the classics, on philosophy and ethics—against community pressures towards vocationalism and specialization. They have done so because they have sometimes had little choice, lacking sufficient priests and lay brothers trained in the sciences; because they have of course a tradition renewed by visits of American clerics to Louvain or Rome; and because the Catholic college, whether run by the diocese or by an order, is less susceptible to direct pressure from lay trustees than comparable Protestant or public colleges. But such insulation is far from complete. The Catholic colleges, expanding to try to cope with the growing multitude of Catholics attending college, desperately need money and often look to wealthy laymen for it. At the same time, in order to keep the best young Catholics within the fold, the colleges must offer them a technical training and chance for general alertness not much inferior to what they could get for less money at the nearest state university; paradoxically, there is some pressure on the Catholic colleges to reduce the diet of the humanities at the same time that the avant-garde nondenominational schools are re-emphasizing the liberal arts. Some Catholic educators have observed, as the result of a number of studies, that even the great Catholic universities such as Notre Dame, Fordham, Catholic University, St. Louis University produce few distinguished scientists (other than physicians), while the record of Catholic scholars in many fields of knowledge remains, in terms of population, relatively meager. Thus, to repair such lacunae of training and of place on the American intellectual map, vigorous priest-educators have inevitably used the model of the leading state and private secular institutions to shame the complacent in their own ranks.

TORPOR IN THE TAIL OF THE PROCESSION

On the other hand, as just indicated, the smaller Catholic colleges have remained, with a few exceptions, relatively unemancipated and eagerly attentive neither to secular nor to European Catholic models. The more liberal-minded on their faculties cannot always count on hierarchical protection against lay anti-intellectualism, and they follow the cosmopolitan Catholicism of *America* or, even less ultra-American, *The Commonweal*, with some apprehensiveness. This is perhaps especially true of some of the small women's colleges where timid Sisters administer for parochially sheltered girls a curriculum ample in dogmatics (and often vocationally oriented towards white-collar jobs like nursing and teaching) but impoverished in many social-science and natural-science areas.[13] While Sisters of cultivation and animation of course exist in such colleges, the contem-

[13] Intense efforts at upgrading are being made in this area: cf. Sister Ritamary, C.H.M., ed., *The Mind of the Church in the Formation of Sisters* (New York: Fordham University Press, 1956). And there are of course colleges for women of high academic standing, e.g., Manhattanville and New Rochelle.

porary battles over academic freedom have largely passed them by (where they have not stood on the sidelines cheering the congressional committees).

As I have already implied, one can find in the tail of the procession Protestant denominational schools, perhaps particularly in the South, which are no less constricting—indeed, which lack the amplitude at least theoretically available to the Catholic teacher. Quite a few of these colleges, relics of earlier denominational zeal, have not been able to obtain accreditation and barely manage to keep alive on small enrollments of children of the faithful; indeed, when the children misbehave, the administration may face financial peril if it fires them.[14] But there are of course enormous differences both within and among the Protestant denominations in terms of the degree and severity of church control, and an imperceptibly diminishing distance separates a college like St. Olaf's, pride of Minnesota's Norwegian Lutherans, or Ohio Wesleyan or Drew (Methodist) from Southern fundamentalist colleges with an enrollment of two or three hundred students from nearby—students whose morals are more actively monitored than their minds.

I have spoken so far mainly of places where there is some life, some movement, even though it may take forms we cannot easily recognize at first glance. But there remain denominational schools which have not sought to become liberal arts colleges, and technical schools and teachers colleges which likewise seem little above the level of the average high school and indeed much inferior to the best high schools. And undoubtedly, as the colleges "above" them and the high schools

[14] This is not a new theme; Andrew White observed it in the last century. See *Autobiography of Andrew D. White* (New York: D. Appleton-Century, 1905); see also Ernest Earnest, *Academic Procession* (Indianapolis: Bobbs-Merrill, 1953), pp. 118–119.

"below" them improve, they must also change or perish, though for a time they can hang on by catering to ever lower intellectual levels and aspirations. In such institutions, the teachers are but hired hands, and their institutions are colleges only by grace of semantic generosity.[15]

Such grace, however, has a double aspect. On the one side, by being called a college, an institution may better claim the airs of academic freedom—much as a patent of nobility, however earned, may give the grantee a certain right to be eccentric. If a group of clerics or businessmen call what they create a "college," they give it at least a potential for upsetting them. But on the other side, by squatting on the title "college," the value of the label is diminished, and higher education becomes to that extent diluted and attenuated. While college ed-

---

[15] Even today, of course, the terms "college" and "university" are not fixed. As we have seen, normal schools are becoming colleges; and colleges, universities, without much control of labelling by the FTC (while established colleges, e.g., Dartmouth, have often felt above the need for upgrading). Still, the levels are much better clarified now than in earlier generations when the nationalization of prestige and semantic fashion had not yet set in. On this topic Bernard Bailyn has written me as follows: "First-rate scholars like Osgood at the end of the 19th century spent large parts of their careers teaching in high schools as a matter of course [I would like to add that in the days before lavish fellowships many scholars taught school to earn money for further study]. By present standards the institutional levels were simply not articulated. . . . Here are a few lines from Neal's *History of New England* (1747 ed.), reporting on a visit to Cambridge and Harvard (italics by me): 'There are several fine streets and good houses in it, besides a flourishing *Academy*, consisting of two spacious *colleges* built of brick, called by the names of Harvard *College* and Stoughton-*Hall*, which are under the government of one president, five fellows, and a treasurer (who) are the immediate governors of the *college*. The learned and ingenious Mr. John Leverett is now president of this *Seminary* . . . . the *Academy* is this year in a very flourishing condition. . . . I have given a particular account of the foundation of this *university*.'"

ucation undoubtedly serves on the whole to raise the
cultural level of America, there is also a counter-tend-
ency in which the unprecedented millions who have de-
manded a college degree have not so much risen as
pulled the colleges down.[16] To be sure, the big state
and private institutions have discovered an appropriate
metabolism for minimizing this: among the former, in-
adequately prepared or motivated freshmen are often
flunked out in great numbers, and the majority of Good-
time Charlies are digested without much pain on either
side, the enzyme being a liberal sprinkling of what was
once the gentleman's "C"—while the more scholarly
professors concentrate on those students who are conscientious or seriously interested in their studies. But,
despite the general growth in student seriousness in the
period since the end of the Second World War, at the

[16] Here again one is struck by the similarity of this development with the problems of the plight of high culture in the face
of middlebrow advance (as discussed by Clement Greenberg,
Ortega y Gassett, Q. D. Leavis, and Dwight Macdonald, *inter
alia*). There is perhaps no inherent reason why mass participation
in the culture (e.g., the extraordinary sales of LP records and
paperback classics, or the rapid spread of avant-garde ideas through
the mass circulation magazines) should threaten high culture
with other than the loss of irrelevant snobbish complacencies
based on coterie prejudices. But the fact is that many producers
of avant-garde work do feel pursued by vulgarization and simpli-
fication, in which all that is difficult, opaque, and intractable in
life and thought is strained out—a process in which what they
consider most important in their work is (to recur to Lasswell's
phrase) restricted by partial incorporation. I have myself come
to feel that it is not only snobbery that leads people to have
misgivings about the easy accessibility of higher education and
higher artistic and intellectual attainments but something of a
genuine concern lest, in our reaction against Puritanism, we throw
out in our cultural life—as we are doing in our occupational life—
whatever is effortful and challenging. Obviously, I cannot in a
footnote begin to deal adequately with issues of such moment,
which I have examined in another perspective in my Founders
Day address at Antioch, *The Oral Tradition, the Printed Word,
and the Screen Image* (Yellow Springs, Ohio: Antioch College
Press, 1955).

tail end of the procession there aren't enough good students to keep their professors alive (the climate remains "collegiate" in the derogatory sense). For the instructors whose community is limited to the local business and professional people in the locality, this presents no problem, for only peripherally would they define themselves as intellectuals. But some of the most bitter and pathetic men I know are those who, trained in a good graduate school, find themselves marooned at such places without the hope or energy of changing their school or their situation. Unless they have enormous self-reliance or the saintliness of the priest whom Georges Bernanos describes in his book, *The Diary of a Country Priest*, all they can do is to go to pot.

American higher education seems to me directionless at the head of the procession as far as major innovations are concerned, in rapid if sometimes contradictory motion in the middle, and lacking in much if any aliveness at the end. The idea of education has successfully infiltrated our national culture nevertheless and taken its place among the accepted powers. Our colleges and universities, however, may be in the situation of the churches today: better attended than ever, bigger and handling more gate receipts, while thoughtful theologians wonder whether religiosity doesn't actually provide an antibody against religion rather than a channel towards it. Education succeeds in emancipating a large proportion of its graduates from provincial roots, only to tie them the more firmly to the big and more subtly constricting orbits of corporate, academic, suburban, and military organizations. With other graduates, higher education lowers its sights in order to avoid despair, and hoping that some culture will rub off on the denizens in four years, often finds that these are only rubbed the wrong way and come out more anti-intellectual than they went in, and better able to throw their weight around. Yet, if I must make an over-all judgment, I am somewhat more impressed with the self-renewing tendencies in academia than depressed by complacent success and mindless stagnation. The spark-producing friction between American life and American universities visibly continues but the sparks, if more reliably produced, are less spectacular.

II

THE INTELLECTUAL
VETO GROUPS

In my previous lecture, we discussed the paradox of abundance, raising questions as to why American higher education, booming and bustling, has lost much of its experimental élan, becoming at once wiser and less exhilarating. We examined the "great chain of being" which connects colleges with each other; indeed, despite the patent lack of any unidimensional basis for discussing academic institutions, we imagined them as a snake-like procession with a turning and twisting head and an imperceptibly moving and elongated tail. In this lecture, our panorama will be somewhat less wide, but our task will be analogous, for we shall be dealing with the social sciences in terms of their competition with each other and in terms of fashionable and prestigeful models among them. The social sciences, in comparison with the rest of academia, are like a Cinderella who has come into splendor. Yet, unlike Cinderella, their situation is a bit disconcerting: they suffer from sudden pangs of abundance, they are unexpectedly courted by the princes of government, industry, and the universities; but the jealous sisters remain a threat and the populace is not wholly sold on this Cinderella's claims.

OBSCURANTISM: OLD AND NEW

Plainly enough, the social scientist shares the general vulnerability of the American intellectual who cannot count on a stratified social order, nor on a dictatorship, to protect him from popular suspicion and resentment. Nor can he count, as the natural philosopher could in the seventeenth century, on the frequently close ties between Puritanism and scientific exploration (ties Robert K. Merton and others have looked into), for the country is steadily less Puritan; moreover, evangelistic fundamentalism, particularly in the South, has been as hostile to science as more intellectual dissenting creeds were supportive. While at the close of the eighteenth century in our seaboard cities an Atlantic culture prevailed (as Carl Bridenbaugh's work shows) in which new fashions in scientific ideas, as well as in clothes and city planning, circulated fast and freely, this merchant and planter insouciance with its support for Franklin, Jefferson, and other deists and freethinkers did not last long; the Enlightenment, which freed masses as well as minds, faltered in its own success. Despite the apparent science-mindedness of Americans, resting largely on technological achievements, obscurantism has been a recurrent power. Many thought it ended with the Scopes trial, when a cocksure and comfortable Mencken could, without afterthought, ridicule Nebraska's Bryan—and when easy use of such digs as "hick" and "hayseed" symbolized the complacency of the sophisticated. Certainly, the fundamentalist Protestant, with his pietism, his evangelism, his Hebraism and insistence on only one Book, the Bible, retreated to the fringes of our national life; far from allying himself with reactionaries among urban Catholics, he was a ready dupe for the Anti-Popery of the Klan. While many Bible colleges remained within the control of such men, it seemed only a matter of time—or urbanization coupled with high-spirited cartooning—before such relics crumbled.

Yet in the last few years many natural scientists have been shocked to discover, often in their own communities, the far from residual power of obscurantism. Medical men have occasionally found anti-vivisectionists (who, as Helen Hughes has suggested, love dogs less than they hate scientists[1]) a real threat. Likewise, the many successes of the opponents of fluoridation of water supplies have startled intellectuals and college professors in a number of small communities. But these fights reveal the new face of obscurantism, as different from Bryan's attitude as Billy Graham is from Elmer Gantry. The new obscurantist does not operate like a parochial hayseed who is at a loss when dealing with city people. He does not come into the open unless he has support from the national media. Thus, the local reactions against alleged pollution of "God's water" were so intense because of support from nationalist right-wingers whose access to communication networks could legitimate the "devout" position and create an opportunity for mobilizing in a tactically effective way all anti-scientific, anti-medical, anti-cosmopolitan anxieties and ferocities (it is irrelevant here that there is some scientific support for anti-fluoridation sentiments). No easy ridicule greets these attacks on science, any more than it greets the attacks, often launched from the same quarters, against "new-fangled notions" in the public

[1] Helen MacGill Hughes, "The Compleat Antivivisectionist," *Scientific Monthly*, vol. 65 (1947), pp. 503–507.

schools; since the rise of Nazism, obscurantism no longer makes us laugh.

The Academic Domestication of Science

To be sure, where more vital matters than tooth decay of nonvoters are at stake, resistance to science is usually futile and scattered: a nice contrast can be made between the strength shown in the fluoridation fights and the weakness of the protests against far greater disturbance of God's water and air by the hydrogen bomb tests. For the most part, the natural scientist doesn't have to defend science as such, either within or without the university (though he may have to defend it against Secretary Wilson's budget-minded thinking about defense and pure research); the Cox and Reece Committees which investigated the Foundations were gunning for the social sciences rather than the natural sciences.

As matters stand today, there are virtually no colleges in this country where natural science is not taught, is not taken for granted. At the avant-garde head of the procession of our academic culture there are, to be sure, renewed rumblings against science on the part of embattled humanists, but the latter aim at best to subdue scientistic arrogance or to vaunt their own, not to censor science as such. And it will be quite a while before their outlook with its complex sources in the work of such men as Aldous Huxley, T. S. Eliot, Joseph Wood Krutch, and Joseph Pieper, and in Buddhistic thought, makes contact with fundamentalist anti-intellectualism at the tail of the procession. On the most backward campuses the engineer who, though he is stuffed full of prejudices, likes to think himself truly scientific is a familiar figure, and Southern California aircraft companies will compete for his services with promises of the full and rounded life.

ECONOMICS: CREATIVE ARENA OF THE
NINETEENTH CENTURY

The social sciences have experienced a different reception. Only recently, indeed, has this term "social science," with its claim to the mantle of science, come into common usage, let alone the still newer term "behavioral sciences," by which the Young Turks of psychology and sociology want to emphasize how scientific they are, how unsocialistic, unscholastic, concerned only with what men *do*, not what they "are."[2] A hundred years ago, with such men as Henry Carey and Francis Lieber, economics and political science began to separate themselves out of moral philosophy, but dealing with human actions and hoping to influence them, it is understandable that they took a long and roundabout time doing so. Whereas Adam Smith could happily be a moralist (his emphasis in *The Theory of Moral Sentiments*) and at the same time an economist (his emphasis in *The Wealth of Nations*), American economists in the Gilded Age often developed a somewhat schizophrenic outlook, illustrated by William Graham Sumner, former minister, zealously insisting on an amoral economic science, or Veblen, passionately oblique reformer, complaining that classical economics had become a normative rather than an evolutionary science. All these social sciences, and particularly sociology, became a decompression chamber for ministers and sons of ministers. In an age of the Social Gospel, the Newtonian desire to penetrate the Divine ground-plan through mechanics

[2] There are of course other motives for the new term; thus, Dr. James G. Miller notes that it provides a link with biology. See, e.g., his paper, "Toward a General Theory for the Behavioral Sciences," in Leonard D. White, ed., *The State of the Social Sciences* (Chicago: University of Chicago Press, 1956), pp. 29–30.

did not disappear, but it set fewer Americans on fire than the desire to grapple with the mysteries of the trusts or the shame of the cities. The fierceness on behalf of an objective Science of some of these pioneers sometimes reflected their having to battle with their own reformist impulses—as well as with a public which, even today, often suspects that socialism (or social work) is the secret spring of the social scientist.

Yet, as part of the same development, the kind of grand metahistorical approach that Vico called the New Science exercised a great attraction for those who wanted something other than the classical curriculum, who sought "life" rather than the laboratory. We can understand why Veblen, philologically trained, went off to study economics at Cornell; why Alvin Johnson, after a classical grounding at Nebraska, sought after the War with Spain to study economics at Columbia; indeed, why a whole generation of iconoclasts did the same. Economics was then less a form of model-building than what it was often in fact called: political economy. It was, along with the Sherman Act and the Wobblies, a response of a once-rural society to the changes brought about by industrialization—changes that could not be understood simply through analyzing the motives of men, but only at least at one remove from motives, by analyzing their exchanges and transactions, by following the flow of goods and credits. Economists, whether radical or conservative in their own motivations, sought to discover the order behind the apparent disorder. In a society of great extremes of wealth, of booms and busts, of trusts and tycoons, economics offered the promise of the greatest intellectual leverage on what was going on, and hence the promise of political and more broadly human relevance. Moreover, that great array of Smith, Ricardo, J. S. Mill, Marx, and Alfred Marshall offered models for emulation, all-embracing systems for security, and enemies for attack—and any field needs all three if it is to capture the gifted and energetic young.

Through the achievements of these men and their disciples in economic analysis, economics could emancipate itself from preachment while not surrendering claims to polity, while political science, perhaps its chief competitor, could only in small part separate itself out from history, philosophy, law, and theology on the one side and rather narrow descriptive or normative accounts of administration and party machinery on the other. Right down to the 1930s, expanding economics departments attracted, *inter alia*, two kinds of students: wouldbe businessmen and managers who saw economics as a bread-and-butter subject,[3] and ambitious intellectuals in search of less palpable forms of mastery. Economics shone, that is, with the reflected glory of its topic: the economy. As economists become more sophisticated, it is clear that for many of them this is only the apparent topic—economic life furnishes merely the concrete examples from which abstraction into mathematical models begins.

Vested Interests versus Economics

As already indicated, economics, or perhaps the type of person who taught economics, did not meet acceptance everywhere. Veblen was refused a post at Lutheran-controlled St. Olaf's College because it was thought he did not believe in God, and today at a good many Cath-

---

[3] Today, a combined engineering and business administration program, which includes some economics, is popular at many universities, being sought out by students less concerned with technological craftsmanship than with managerial aims. There is of course an enormous gap between such a program at MIT (with economics à la Samuelson) and at many A & M colleges or others where low-level "applied" economics is taught by business school professors.

olic colleges it is my impression that economics is still under dogmatic wraps, being taught in part from the Encyclicals as a branch of moral philosophy, this being one of the instances where the tail of the procession often makes unsuspecting contact with the avant-garde groups who want to restore the role of values in the social sciences, including economics. Up until recently, moreover, businessmen trustees occasionally didn't want economic analysis taught, either because they regarded it as impractical or as potentially critical and reformist. Classicists, philologists, and philosophers frequently regarded economists as vulgar fellows, hardly a step above "trade." Furthermore, in part because the initial steps in economic theory are a bit forbidding, economics never got into most secondary schools, and hence is even now absent from the curricula of many teachers colleges (though some of its less abstract concerns reappear there in geography and social studies programs).

THE APPEAL OF THE "NEWER" SOCIAL SCIENCES

On the whole, however, while economics is still being assimilated in the rear parts of the procession, it has been losing its interest for the head of it. Its place is challenged by what, for the sake of brevity, I shall call the "newer" social sciences, which include anthropology, sociology, and social psychology, as against the older trinity of economics, history, and political science. These newer fields can, of course, when in search of ancestors, trace themselves back to some eminent Greek, but they are newer in the sense of late entry into European or European-style departments of law, philosophy, or economics; and they frequently exhibit the behavior of newcomers in their anxious concern for their independence, professional standing, and intellectual specific gravity.

The spread of these new fields has been so rapid that, for example, thoughtful anthropologists are worrying lest their tradition of field-work as a novitiate be quietly scrapped because graduate students without Ph.D.s can now get jobs as assistant professors at colleges which are inaugurating an anthropology department or want to add an anthropologist as an essential ingredient in a general education program. Government bureaus, moreover, which once had places only for lawyers, economists, and statisticians, are now hiring the newer breeds to help train Point IV technicians, or to study leadership in the Army, or for a plethora of other missions. Law schools, which once thought themselves heretical to hire economists (as Yale hired Walton Hamilton, or Chicago the late Henry Simon and Aaron Director), are now casting about for sociologists. And because the newer social sciences can easily be watered down, there is no college so near the end of the procession as not to be able to come to terms with them in some fashion, as many high and grammar schools have discovered in amalgamating history with social studies.[4]

Opposition to the Newer Fields

The watering down I refer to here is not merely in terms of intellectual density but also of critical detachment from current fanaticisms. Yet the xenophobes are

[4] It is easy, of course, for the university professor to poke fun at social studies in the secondary schools—and he is perhaps especially prone to do so when he sees the complexities, which are his daily frontier, shabbily oversimplified. What he is likely to forget is that at many schools social studies, no matter how badly taught, may do less damage than the patrioteering history they replace or amplify; they may even be the one spark of life in a moribund curriculum. The point is further dealt with in my third lecture, pp. 127 et seq.

It is obvious, moreover, that the university-based critic of "edu-

right to fear the social studies, even in a 3.2% or local option concentration, for those who have been exposed at least at the graduate level to anthropological perspectives can only rarely be counted on as safe-and-sound home-guardists. Whereas I have run into a number of politically reactionary professors in economics departments—sometimes teaching accounting or marketing or business law—a truly reactionary anthropologist is, in my experience, a very rare bird indeed. There is some paradox here, for the anthropologist's credo has been cultural relativism, a credo which often can lead to defense of custom as such, and thus, if never to reaction, at least to an oblique defense of the status quo and certainly to a defense of sympathetic understanding of reactionaries or any other cultural group. At the same time, as part of this credo, the anthropologist must oppose any cultural group's assumption of superiority, especially if on racist grounds, and this often puts him at odds not only with Southern advocates of white supremacy but with chauvinist advocates of American supremacy. An anthropologist may be willing to defend inequality and privilege in an African kingdom or an American county, but committed as he is to the principle of culture as such, he will insist that the African kingdom has as much right to its way of life as we have to ours—and, compared with the United States, the African kingdom is the underdog. Parochial in its traditional topics, the discipline is inherently cosmopolitan

---

cationists" often does not bother to understand the enemy he is attacking, considering it beneath him to examine the rapidly changing curricula of teacher-training institutions. Even at the Stanford Conference of educators and anthropologists reported in *Education and Anthropology*, several anthropologists seemed almost to parade as a virtue their ignorance of such curricula—much as a patriarch would parade his ignorance of "women's work." This is all the more striking because the Conference is notable for its sympathy with the problems of teachers and teachers colleges.

in its effects, and hence would seem bound, as it travels down toward the end of the procession, to become involved in conflict.

That this has not actually happened to a greater extent may in part be due to the training anthropologists, as well as many sociologists, get in maintaining rapport in a field situation. That may mean no more than keeping one's mouth shut on principle rather than out of cowardice, but such a principle is often a help to a discipline whose outposts have outrun its entrenched sources of protection. One could argue, moreover, that American anthropologists in dealing with this country —for instance, Margaret Mead, Lloyd Warner, James West (the author of *Plainville, U.S.A.*)—have been rather more charitable than comparable sociologists— for instance, the Lynds, or C. Wright Mills; and yet in either case to look at the customs of our country in the same way as at those of a preliterate tribe may shock even those who have learned to endure having the economy studied or the city manager plan discussed in the classroom. The very intimacy which has made the newer social sciences appealing to many among the young loosens the protective mantle of Science and appears to those of rigid mind as socially dangerous because of its apparently unaseptic atmosphere of inquiry. Moreover, while Americans have had a hundred years to learn that economics, for all its revolutionary offshoots and implications, hasn't done anything worse than raise the national debt—dreadful as that is!—anthropology and sociology stand today where economics once did, with as yet unfathomed possibilities for, as some might put it, "subverting the young."[5]

[5] That barbaric document, the Reece Committee Report on Foundations, is full of evidence of the fears that the newer social sciences arouse. The very largest foundations have often quite courageously backed the newer social sciences—and it will take still more courage after the attacks on the Fund for the Republic

and the Ford Foundation. These attacks have been more frightening than earlier attacks, e.g., on Rockefeller, because, in threatening to remove tax exemption, they struck at the heart of capitalist prerogative (an ironical move for self-styled conservatives); the same is true of the campaign waged against Ford and Mercury cars (which led the dealers to put pressure on Henry Ford II)—the rich no longer can afford to be eccentric even at one remove; another sign of the loss of the social-class protections which once operated to support scientific speculation and intellectual irreverence.

Those foundations which have backed the social sciences have followed the Flexner formula that foundation money should be pilot money; they have done so because these sciences are new. Thus, while economists have now got government and business collecting their data for them, psychologists and sociologists have not yet successfully institutionalized the gathering of the sorts of data they want. (For instance, we have very little data on how leisure is spent compared to what we have on work and production.) Gathering data is very expensive, and thus grants to the newer social sciences can sometimes be both massive and strategic.

It would make a fascinating, if dispiriting, study of the intellectual veto groups to compare the brave new charter the Ford Foundation published in 1949—the report of its study committee—with its accomplishments since. The original document was a radical prospectus, with its high hopes for peace, prosperity, and good will through applied social science. In a few areas (among them: the Fund for the Republic, some phases of school and adult education, some grants in the social sciences) these imperatives have retained a fair amount of their original force; but in many others —notably, the pious largesse for faculty salaries—caution and academicism rapidly defeated impetuosity. Only the most oblique relation remains with the starting point, so that one can no longer often tell, from the nature of a program (as against its size), whether Ford or Carnegie or one of the other major foundations in the social science area is the sponsor. This is not said to join in the specific jibes and criticisms scored by Dwight Macdonald in his New Yorker series, for the Ford Foundation administrators found little enough professional support for the innovative aims the Foundation began with; in its early days, it offended many sacred traditions of ponderous donors, and was quickly made to feel vulnerable both in its academic and its wider constituencies. Like many young people today, who become sophisticated in their early teens, it became "mature" all too quickly.

The Student "Vote"

At the same time, as part of the same development we have been discussing, there has occurred at many of the leading universities a profound shift in the interests of the students. At the University of Michigan (cf. Logan Wilson's *The Academic Man*), a course in abnormal psychology has been the only one which students unequivocally liked, and in the College at Chicago a course in "culture and personality," so the gossip has it, has probably been the most popular one. (Unlike Michigan, we don't do explicit consumer research on our students—in a monopolistic program, one doesn't need to!) Sociology is still thought to be a gut course for the football team at many schools (a view sometimes unjust to the football team, if not to sociology), but it is not only that reputation which makes it attractive. Among thoughtful students in the postwar years, there has developed a preoccupation with private life, with human relations rather than international relations. Thus, while some students enter anthropology or sociology who would once have gone into law, politics, or economics—that is, to better the world or their position in it—many others enter the more social social sciences in order to better their understanding of themselves. For them, the economy is simply part of the given, of the landscape; so, for that matter, are wars and rumors of wars. From the perspective of many in the older generation, it looks as if these students have retreated from the implacabilities of the great world—and from the disciplines which seek to master these implacabilities—into the more malleable areas of personal and social life. On the other hand, the young, feeling often that their zealot elders have staked out all political positions—and that these are irrelevant anyway to a world of barely ruffled war prosperity—have preferred to concentrate on what appears to the adolescent as the inexhaustible frontier of personal relations, and on the disciplines which promise an understanding of them.

A year ago there came across my desk a very curious document. It was a mimeographed attack by a colleague at Chicago, an economist, on our undergraduate social science program on the ground, *inter alia*, that out of it came fewer majors in economics than in the "base years" 1934–40 before the new college program (whereas today more majors went into sociology, human development, psychology, and so on). Although he had to recognize that this is a general phenomenon, he hammered away at our "culture and personality" course as a kind of Pied Piper, somehow seducing the young—presumably by talk of such enticing matters as sex and social class. It was amusing to find an economist who professes a belief in free trade asking in effect for an intellectual tariff or parity. We might call his reaction "disciplinary" home-guardism as against "regional" home-guardism. Similar attacks greeted the rise of the Department of Social Relations at Harvard which, formed in 1946, was within two years third in student enrollment. In recognizing the concerns of the post-war students, the Harvard administration was merely giving one further illustration of the democratization of that university, its refusal to hold a snobbish fort for the humanities and the older social sciences (cf., e.g., Conant's *Education in a Divided World*, Chapter 6), and by the same token its attention to trends in the nation at large.

Indeed, the sheer fact of tremendous increase in enrollments at many universities has unsettled traditional tacit treaties among the disciplines, for the increase has brought new cadres of students from different places, different strata, and different types of high schools—students often unaware of, or unintimidated by, the universities' given roster of departmental affiliations. While the students have not on the whole acted as lobbies for ideological systems or for professors committed to such systems (a point I return to shortly), their very presence has been an element in the pressure for establishing new fields which could attract majors. Other more marginal constituencies have operated to the same effect, such as adults attending night school or taking correspondence courses, or teachers in summer school or wartime officer candidates.

These pressures, as I have said, have been more often responded to by the president, with his brain trust of the more adventurous and cosmopolitan professors, and resisted by the often accidental collocation of old-line departments. The result has sometimes been, as at Chicago, to create a structure resembling that of Roosevelt's New Deal Administration: old-line departments were not abolished, but an overlapping jurisdiction was given a new agency, such as an interdisciplinary committee. Only rising enrollments and even more rapidly rising budgets can prevent jurisdictional dispute from becoming a major activity under such conditions.

ANTHROPOLOGY AND ITS ALLIES AS THE
CREATIVE ARENA OF TODAY

In my opinion, the coming of the newer social sciences, whatever they imply for a slackening of political reformism and whatever their potential for laxity in tepid social studies programs, has on the whole made for cultural vitality and liberation. But, as with other avant-garde ideas, the general acceptance of a novel approach soon reduces its power. Ideas are like a general prosperity built on inflation—we soon get used to the new level of living and it no longer excites (or disorients) us. With intellectual experiences as with other capital equipment, we need to earn them for ourselves and are not much helped by mere inheritance. And much of the attraction of the newer social sciences springs from the fact, dismaying to many, that they do not consist simply of a cumulative series of discoveries, as in the natural sciences, but that they are also a method of self-exploration which is noncumulative, which dies with every explorer or with each generation of explorers. We can accept on hearsay that there are atoms or exploding universes; we cannot take on faith the existence of the unconscious or even of the power of culture (though faith may encourage us to look for evidence in and around ourselves). This, incidentally, is one reason why at many colleges today anthropology and sociology are more open and humanistic than the regular humanities departments, for whom the disciplinary map of existence appears to be a known thing.

The End of Liberation?

Even so, with the widespread acceptance of psychoanalytic and cultural modes of thinking,[6] the newer social sciences have lost at many institutions a good deal of the air of discovery that still makes them attractive elsewhere. And we can imagine quite a few of today's high school youngsters, coming to college after overexposure to the social studies and already possessed of a certain poise in their social relations, finding diminished excitement in exploring these relations intellectually. Conceivably, such students may in college reject the so-

[6] Psychoanalysis, "old stuff" as it seems to be among wide educated strata, is actually taken for granted only among a small fraction even of the college-going population; Shirley Star's Mental Health Study for the National Opinion Research Center indicates that (in 1950) barely 2% of adult Americans had sympathy for or grasp of any kind of psychotherapeutic approach.

cial sciences as a whole, and look for sustenance in the humanities or outside the curriculum altogether.

Moreover, not only have the social sciences gained a certain acceptance among educated people, but they have also become pragmatically important. The Extension Services have long carried agricultural economics and rural sociology to the farmer, while the President's Council of Economic Advisors institutionalizes an economic theory which a few years ago was considered radical. At some of our major universities, the social sciences are as wrapped up in the defense effort as the physics and chemistry departments are: the atmosphere of Cold War of some leading departments, whose faculty members have frequent contact with CIA or the Rand Corporation or other like agencies, is quite different from that in a traditional Ivy League college.

Where the "Newer" Sciences Are Still New

I have been concentrating here on that small minority of institutions where social research is done, or is supposed to be done, and indicating how the newer social sciences, suddenly thrust into the big leagues and the limelight, have lost some of the leverage which a fringe enterprise has to introduce new styles and methods. But in the middle and tail of the procession neither fat government contracts nor entrenched research traditions rob these fields of the hazards and glories of pioneering. And whereas a generation ago, as we have seen, economics was the vessel of dissent at many of these schools, it is in the newer social sciences that dissent stirs, that off-beat students are attracted who want to grapple with life as they experience it, and not as the disciplines divide it and measure it out.

These may be among the type of students described

in a recent study by the sociologist Robin Williams, Jr.;
he declares that these students:

> seem to be more interested in what they get *out* of a
> job than what they get *for* it. They are particularly in-
> terested in the gratifications to be derived from per-
> sonal relationships. Many choose a particular occupa-
> tion because "it will give me a chance to help people"
> or "I like people." . . . Almost one-sixth of the stu-
> dents think the main importance of the college lies in
> teaching them how to use their "personalities" to
> achieve success in working with people. (*Quarterly
> Report*, Carnegie Corporation, Oct. 1955, vol. 3,
> no. 4.)

Neither for high motives nor for low ones will such
students think economics the answer to their needs, although they may find, when they enter psychology
courses, for instance, that the style of thinking is not
so different from economics and, save in the clinical
courses, the answers to their very personal questions very
tangentially forthcoming, if at all.

MOVEMENTS TOWARDS INTEGRATION

On the whole, however, the disciplines have drawn
people in with some selectivity, so that those interested
in personal relations have not gone into economics or
history, and those interested in the theory of the firm
have not gone into social psychology.[7] This is so despite
the fact that every field harbors within it greater differ-

[7] Anne Roe in *The Making of a Scientist* has used Rorschach
and other personality tests to draw the profiles of various "types"
of (mostly natural) scientists. Cf. my exploratory discussion of
Veblen's motivations in *Thorstein Veblen: A Critical Interpre-
tation* (New York: Scribner's, 1953), Chapter 1.

ences than those which divide it, on the average, from neighboring fields. While people in search of a clear identity would like to be able to say that there is only one kind of political science or only one kind of sociology or economics, this will never be so, given the vagaries of careers and recruitment, as well as the protean nature both of theory and of data. An enterprising dean, however, worried about the things that get left out between fields and about the slowness of interchange among them, may seek to promote interdisciplinary programs in order to mix the new with the old faster than would occur through intellectual osmosis within his faculty. Such a dean doesn't see why the faculty should hear of each other's work only through students they have in common or an occasional book they have read in common. Sometimes what he does about it he labels general education, sometimes not; I am speaking here only of social science programs, and not of those for which the social sciences themselves are too narrow a box.

"Restriction through Partial Incorporation" Again

But we should stop a moment and look at the latter problem. Where, as at Chicago, the social sciences are grouped together, the result can be an increased communication and fluidity within the grouping, but a somewhat lessened communication outside it. A sociologist who is brought together with psychologists, for instance, may not necessarily see less of philosophers, and the psychologists not necessarily less of biologists—for in human affairs the principle of "the more, the more" usually operates—but at the same time he will have an alibi for cutting off other contacts if he wants. And within the social sciences, too, the integration programs sometimes have a similarly mixed effect. One finds general social science courses, for example, which present in a single package history, government, and economics, sometimes localized to America or the Western World. Other packages bring together anthropology, sociology, and psychology. If we look at the latter, we can see that there are enough terminological and stylistic distinctions among the three disciplines to keep unifiers busy for several generations; and what we find in practice is frequently a course jointly taught by members of three departments, all competing for majors or graduate students, while at the same time making efforts, more or less valiant or successful, to adopt a joint conceptual frame —at worst a sort of pidgin English, with, for instance, psychologists learning to say "culture" or "social structure" from time to time; at best ascetic adoption of terms derived from some overarching scheme like that of Talcott Parsons. What Freud termed "narcissism with respect to minor differences" can preoccupy such a faculty indefinitely.

Similarly, professors of government forced to work with economists may develop a course on government control of business (or on business control of government), though losing on the way most of the technical virtuosity of economic analysis. But they can keep busy at this indefinitely: the problems are real ones. The result, however, tends to be that each such group feels that the boundaries of its intellectual task are set by the difficulties with the neighboring tribes—not by the difficulties with the tribes not present at their conference table. We see here again the dialectic of parish and nation—only we see that there are many parishes within parishes. If one thinks, as I do, that the relations between the older and the newer social sciences are the really decisive ones for the future of both groups, then one may feel that the achievement of a modest integration between sociology and psychology, or government and economics, may actually delay the more significant attempt at integrating economics and psychology or anthropology and history.

HISTORY AND ANTHROPOLOGY: A CASE
STUDY IN ACCULTURATION

Collaborations of this sort, however, are made difficult, not only by the accidental inheritances of departmental boundaries, but also by the temperamental differences between representative men in the several fields; the differences in initial recruitment are exacerbated by graduate training with its pressure for the assumption of a new professional identity. To illustrate this theme, I could use many examples[8] of collaboration I have been party to or witnessed; let me select some of the things that happen when historians and anthropologists try to work together. For the purposes of my account, I shall create an "ideal-typical" member of each discipline and assume that he gets interested in the materials and personnel of the other field.

The Historian's Preconceptions

Each will begin, first of all, with an image of the other person which is in part a refraction of the self-image he has as a member of his own group. Thus, our fictional historian sees the social scientist, in general, as an uncultivated person, without knowledge of, let alone rev-

[8] In *The Open Mind* (New York: Simon and Schuster, 1955), pp. 121–123, J. Robert Oppenheimer speaks of the differences in style among physicists, mathematicians, and chemists—a topic to which my colleague Richard Meier has devoted much attention. Chemists, of course, are too huge and differentiated a group to maintain a common culture, but theoretical physicists have approximated one. Cf. Reuel Denney, "The Scientific Corps—A Sixth Estate?" *Confluence*, vol. 3 (1954), pp. 220–229.

erence for, the past. His vulgarity appears in his putting himself forward in what he writes—his often self-conscious effort to declare his own values, his own biases; in contrast to this, the historian tends to minimize the role of his own self, of his own projectivity if not his selectivity, so that even a Collingwood, no *echt*-historian, is gingerly in handling a personal anecdote. (A nice example turned up the other day when a historian was talking to a seminar largely composed of sociologists. He told us how he had happened to study Latin-American cities, and then apologized for the surely not tasteless revelation.) Moreover, the historian sees the anthropologist (and his allies among the *novi homines* of behavioral science) as able by grandiose talk to capture students and foundations, leaving historians to hold hands with professors of Greek; by the same token, anthropologists have the ear of governments, always flying to Washington or Micronesia, or advising market researchers—promoters rather than scholars. Yet there is ambivalence in this disdain. These new men must have something. They talk a lot about methods—so much so that one of their number was recently heard to exclaim: "Oh dear, why can't we just go out and *do* ethnography the way we used to." They know a lot of jargon which is villainous enough, but impenetrable; they know about Rorschach tests, interviewing, and even sampling.

Perils of the Foot-loose Historian

What happens then to the historian who is venturesome enough and attracted enough to try to cross the boundary? He will tend to assume that, since he has the older and higher academic status, the anthropologists he comes among will welcome him with open arms, that they will be grateful for his discovering them. But anthropologists are quite as proud as historians, and perhaps more polemical. In the past at least, they have often been men and women of some means and status who have felt more at home with the chiefs of a preliterate tribe than with commoners in their own country. Until people started revisiting Tepotzlán, the anthropologist was as securely in command of "his" adopted culture as any historian who had taken for his moated terrain the history of Macedonia in the first century B.C. or the intellectual life of Milwaukee between the Mexican and the Civil Wars. Moreover, as already indicated, the peer-group of the anthropologist, for the most part, is confined to the newer social sciences; unless he is archaeologically inclined, or of unusually humanistic bent, he won't know enough about what historians think of him to be grateful for an exception.

But the historian's troubles have only begun at this point. The anthropologists he has heard of, the popularized ones, are, he assumes, also the ones whom their colleagues hold in high esteem; then he discovers, to his dismay, that the tight in-groups of anthropology often share the prejudices he is fleeing, only more so. I have seen it happen a number of times that historians attracted by the work of Margaret Mead or Ruth Benedict or Lloyd Warner are told by other anthropologists with whom they have on that account made contact that these anthropologists are not to be trusted.[9] Who then

---

[9] In his introduction to a volume reporting the proceedings of a conference which brought educationists and anthropologists together, Professor George D. Spindler, an anthropologist, reports on his survey of which anthropologists are considered to be "anthropology" by textbook writers in the field of education. He declares: "A frequency-of-citation chart for the literature examined reveals that Kluckhohn, Mead, Benedict, [Allison] Davis, West (Carl Withers), and Warner are cited in great disproportion to all others. . . . Particularly significant is the fact that it is the relatively most popularized works of these contributors that are cited most frequently. . . . the educators are not getting a fair and substantial diet of anthropological materials. This will only change

is a sound ethnographer? At this point the historian may
find himself plunged into a disquisition on the differences between British social anthropology and American cultural anthropology—or any one of a hundred
such topics in the repertory of any discipline. As his be-
wilderment grows, he will be told in effect: why don't
you go back where you came from—go back at least
until you are willing to spend two or three years learning
these fine points of the trade.

Man on a Margin

A more general phenomenon is at work in this hazing
given to the newcomer, one which we can observe in
many diverse situations of contact among groups. For
instance, the American who travels abroad is, ordinarily,
more sympathetic to foreigners and less ethnocentric
than the American who stays home; but abroad he is
taken as *the* American and is belabored by his hosts for
all the sins, real and alleged, of his countrymen, sins of
which he has often been highly critical. (To be sure,
at home he may not have been considered a real American in all quarters, and he may find a certain ironic
satisfaction in "passing" as one abroad.) Likewise, I
have seen Southern students at Northern colleges put
on the defensive because they were not willing to dis-
own, on any and all occasions, Southern race attitudes,
though some of these students left the South because

---

when the educators take the next step and get their hands dirty
with some of the dust-laden monographs back in the stacks, and
when anthropologists exhume their portfolios of esoteria and put
them into more publicly usable form." Spindler, ed., *Education
and Anthropology* (Stanford: Stanford University Press, 1955),
p. 18. Involved in this feeling that the subtleties and varieties of
anthropology are diminished by transmission across disciplinary
boundaries are some of the same attitudes indicated in my first
lecture (see footnote 16, on p. 63) concerning transmission of
high culture across social-class and "brow" boundaries.

they did not wholly share those attitudes. Lacking perspective, people are apt to take the nearest person in their field of vision as a reminder of or scapegoat for the very group he has left—a group which will probably never hear of the blows he suffers on its behalf; it is as if his physical presence resembles a hostage's more than a guest's. (I need hardly add that, as someone who has traveled among the disciplines rather than stayed home, I have experienced a good deal of this myself, with the strain on loyalties it engenders, as when among students and teachers in the humanities I am made a stand-in for all they find inhumane or power-hungry in the social sciences.) Any person with experience in sectarian religious or political life has had similar encounters with members of sects close to his own but not identical.

Experiencing such a reception, the historian may be tempted to go home again, but he may have misgivings about it. For he probably shares the conviction which we have seen to be needed by many academic people—that what one is doing is a bit, or more than a bit, heretical. The historian has thought accordingly that he was very bold indeed to have truck with the illiterates who study preliterates; he has conjured up visions of being read out of his own trade union, of having burned his bridges. Actually, of course, the other historians are neither that interested nor that venomous nor that united, but having this image, the wanderer will feel at times that he is a man without a country. A sad plight, indeed, especially for an historian.

The Anthropologist's Preconceptions

If we turn now to the other side of the boundary, we see that the anthropologist also has his picture of the historian. He may see him as over-bookish, a donnish person in a Gothic tower. If he is not in the humanistic wing of anthropology—a strong wing, as Kroeber's work shows, even while he criticizes it—he may associate historians with all the snobbish people who claim culture as their word and their world. The behavioral scientist may not write as well as the historian nor read as much. Perhaps he may also feel that the historian is more secure in his method; his informants are dead. And, until recently, he might also feel that historians are in control of the big and important powers, while he is confined to the inconsequential and disappearing outlanders—much as sociologists until recently could not touch the economy which belonged to the economists and could not touch government and military affairs which belonged to the political scientists, but had to find their clientele among criminals, children, old people, immigrants, factory workers, small-town folk, and other relatively powerless groups whom no one else had laid claim to.

What happens, then, when the anthropologist leaves his peer-group to try to work with historians? As a student of culture and subculture, he is more likely than the historian to have cased the others' joint before venturing into it, and so he is apt to be in for fewer surprises. Moreover, there has been a growing tendency in anthropology itself to seek historical reconstructions as well as synchronic cross-sections wherever the conditions of field work permit; some anthropologists have even revived a moderate and chastened form of evolutionism, and many are preoccupied with historically focused studies of culture change and acculturation. A certain happy eclecticism or omnivorousness survives in anthropology from the days of one-man expeditions. Despite this, anthropologists may still encounter severe conflicts when they venture among the historians. The historian is often a person whose job it is to destroy the other fellow's generalization. To take a noted instance, historians in the past half-century have written a whole library which takes exception to Max Weber's essay on the Protestant Ethic with such comments as, "however in Florence in 1204, such and such," or "in Flanders in 1627 the Catholics were heavily engaged in the most rationalized segments of the wool trade." Your true historian will boggle at such a lay term as the Renaissance, pushing its origins ever back into what used to be called the Dark Ages, so that one sometimes gathers from reading history that nothing ever changes since it always has a precursor. This is very hard going for those anthropologists or other behavioral scientists who seek generalizations; to be sure not all anthropologists define science as generalization, being satisfied with descriptive ethnography.

Perils of the Ambitious Anthropologist

More conflict-laden is a second possibility, namely that the anthropologist will want to share with the historian his access to the big powers as well as to keep his monopoly of the small ones. When the Columbia University Research on Contemporary Cultures started, under anthropological leadership, to study, not Palau and the Tiv or the Hopi, but France, China, and the Soviet Union, and when the Russian Research Center started under Clyde Kluckhohn's direction, many historians and their allies among the older disciplines were bitterly resentful. They seized upon Gorer's swaddling theory with fierce and, I think, disproportionate, indignation. At the Conference on Totalitarianism held at the Academy of Arts and Sciences in 1953, some able scholars could not contain their fury when social-psychological or configurational interpretations were offered for Soviet behavior. Many anthropologists, too, have been told to go back where they came from.

But possibility of return tends to be cut off, in part by

ambivalence among the anthropologists themselves towards the forays some of them are making into affairs of
state. Indeed, the shining simplicity of the earlier forms
of ethical relativism has been a casualty of this development. As many observers have pointed out, it was all
very well to seek neutrality towards the exotic behavior
of the vanishing Dobuans or Nanda—but not towards
the racist behavior of the Nazis or the suppression of
cultural pluralism and the extirpation of whole peoples
in the Soviet Union. Big power problems brought big
power ethical dilemmas, including *raison d'état*, and the
anthropologist who is now "debriefed" in the CIA or
the State Department after a visit to the Laplanders or
an Indonesian village feels he is losing the foot-loose in-
nocence that allowed American field workers to remain
(compared with British ones) quite "un-royal" until the
Second World War.

Splintering of the Anthropologists' Small-Group Ethos

Before that time, anthropologists—a relatively small
group, as I have earlier remarked—could feel they shared
the common culture of having been in the field, of having had to face alone, or virtually so, often unnerving
problems of grappling with a strange tongue, sometimes
disquieting ways, and an opaque social structure, problems sensitively portrayed in Elenore Smith Bowen's *Return to Laughter*. As Richard Pope has pointed out to
me, it may well be that anthropologists did not always
appreciate fully how various this *rite de passage* was, at
least outside certain American Indian groups: on the
surface, the problems of field work bore similar labels,
and each returned traveler could talk about "his" tribe
in seemingly consensual terms, creating a greater impression of the uniformity of encounters than was warranted
—or blaming themselves privately as individuals for dif-

ferences, especially unhappy ones, in their own experiences. Once, however, people began to do "field work" in literate communities, or in semiliterate ones like "Plainville, U.S.A.," let alone working in New York City with foreign films and foreign-born informants, the illusion of a common anthropological culture created by a common and taxing experience tended to break down.

In danger of being lost under these changed conditions is the traditional anthropological conviction that we can learn as much from a small power that has no navy, no archives, and only an embryonic elite as from the big ones that make and consume headlines and psychological warfare. Indeed, cultural relativism has included among its non-relativistic assumptions the passionate belief that each power, irrespective of size or ability to threaten or be exploited, counts one: an international democracy of one culture, one vote. As Margaret Mead put it (in a comment at the Stanford Conference reported in *Education and Anthropology*): "One of the basic assumptions that anthropologists have worked with has been that you treat each culture as dignified in itself; it's a kind of theoretical democracy among cultures—granting that the Eskimo did things very simply and the Peruvians did them very complicatedly." While as I have said anthropologists are often criticized—with justice, I think, but without mercy—for "ignoring history," it has been an achievement of their profession to ignore merely contemporary rankings either of territories or of problems. The consequence is that anthropologists at work, usually under government subsidy, at the interdisciplinary frontier of Soviet and other big-power studies of national culture and character can be hurt not only by the attacks they meet from the already entrenched but by the fact that they have internalized many values which make them vulnerable in terms of their own discipline.

Natives' Return

Indeed, anthropological work on culture contact helps us to see some of the consequences of such confrontation. Where a minority group seeks acceptance at the hands of a powerful majority, it opens up its own ethical system to strain but does not abandon it. Strictures by the majority may then reverberate with a double potency since they are received in terms of the newly accepted majority values plus the still encapsulated minority ones. Thus, where native peoples on shouldering the white man's burden have found themselves not treated as fully white, there has often been observed a nativist reaction—a reaction analogous to the "third generation" reaction of American ethnic groups noted some years ago by the historian Marcus Hansen. The old values which are then returned to are altered by the very process of self-conscious return; thus, they are espoused with a chauvinism whose techniques and tenets are often taken over from the majority. I believe we can detect something like a nativist or third-generation reaction in anthropology, as well as in a number of the other newer disciplines which have suffered frustration in attempts at integration. There has been a movement in anthropology away from the culture-and-personality school, a renewed preoccupation with special methodologies, an almost pathetic eagerness to show that anthropologists of either sex are as tough-minded, hardheaded scientists as any critic from another discipline could ask.

If one traces descent from Franz Boas, one might speak quite literally of a third-generation reaction. Many of Boas' students broke away from this awesome old-country patriarch—though it was hard to find a direction in which he had not pioneered. But their students in turn are often the ones who have become pious towards the ancestral memories. I recall a student of Ruth Benedict's telling me a year or so ago how much he regretted having been encouraged by her to experiment with psychological tests; if only he'd been trained by a straight and narrow ethnographer, he felt he would have had a clearer, less conflict-ridden self-image. Back to the fold, and no more hyphenated anthropology for him.

THE EMOTIONAL FRONTIER OF COLLABORATION

Similar things have happened even where the disciplines seeking integration have all been of the newer breeds, as in the Department of Social Relations at Harvard or the Committee on Human Development at Chicago. In both cases, while the pioneering professors continue to wander at will, the students now coming along sometimes seek refuge in a disciplinary third-generation identity at the first signs of nonacceptance of newly invented or marginal identities, and these experimental departments oscillate between Balkanization and overserious straining for an imperial unity. Such, I would suppose, is the dialectic of all but the most utopian culture-contact situations, at least in the social sciences. For it is my impression that, despite the differences in status and style that exist among the physical and biological sciences, their problems of collaboration are somewhat less grave. Since they are not themselves the subjects of their own research, their motives for becoming researchers can perhaps remain more opaque; teamwork has a longer tradition and its problems of priority, performance, and responsibility are a bit more prepared for; and, while expensive failure is still a disaster to a rising social science, it is taken for granted as the luck of the game in much natural science research.[10] Two psychiatrists who have had experience in joint projects both with natural and with behavioral scientists conclude that there is more unconscious guilt and anxiety in the work of the latter, with consequently greater strain in interdisciplinary adventures which threaten the rituals and defenses built up against the inner conflicts. "This hypothesis," they declare, "implies that even when different motivations can be reconciled—for instance, by the relative similarity of scientific backgrounds, or by a common goal—the joint motivation cannot be as strong as the motivation of a single investigator. . . . A command performance at the behest of an administrative head of a project can rarely evoke the narcissism of the individual investigators. Only identification with a 'scientific' leader can bring into play these narcissistic forces."[11] Their observations clarify and confirm mine (including my not always consoling self-observations as a member of interdisciplinary teams), and give some basis in individual psychology for the group-contact reactions I have been discussing.

[10] On the other hand, these differences should not be overestimated. For observant discussion of hysterical pressure for results, stemming from careerist opportunism in biological science, see the presidential address of Austin M. Brues before the American Association for Cancer Research, "The New Emotionalism in Research," Cancer Research, vol. 15 (1955), pp. 345–353.

[11] See Fredrick C. Redlich and Eugene B. Brody, "Emotional Problems of Interdisciplinary Research in Psychiatry," Psychiatry, vol. 18 (1955), pp. 233–239, at p. 235. In a perceptive article, my colleague, R. Richard Wohl, notes similar emotional blocks to interdisciplinary research, and stresses the role of the tactful administrator in minimizing anxiety and defensiveness among collaborators. "Some Observations on the Social Organization of Interdisciplinary Social Science Research," Social Forces, vol. 33, 1955, pp. 374–383.

DIFFERENT MEANINGS OF INTEGRATION AT THE
HEAD AND TAIL OF THE PROCESSION

Do these considerations and experiences imply that all steps toward integration are inevitably self-defeating, leading to the replacement of one scholarly nationalism by another, even if a larger and more inclusive one? Some such dialectic of advance and retreat is undoubtedly present. But perspective requires taking account of two other things which are also present. One is recognition that the more productive of the new groupings may and often should become new specialities in a continuous process of fission and reunion. The kaleidoscope of possible combinations is, I suspect, a good deal richer than we ordinarily think.

The second consideration requires us to look again, not at the avant-garde institutions which have experimented with mixing the disciplines, but at the entire length of our metaphorical snake. The movement towards integration of specialties means different things at different academic levels. The top schools, which once led the parade towards graduate training and specialization, have also included those which initiated the movement away from a rigid departmentalism, as for example, the Contemporary Civilization courses in the '20s at Columbia, or Meiklejohn's Experimental College at Wisconsin, or the general education courses at Chicago and Harvard. Today, the old isolationist type of disciplinary "nationalism" is rarer at the major institutions, where leading figures count themselves interdisciplinary to some degree. To be sure, they often do so for imperialist reasons, because each sees "his" field as the core field and the other areas as tributary.[12] But his

[12] Cf. the paper by my colleague, Calvin Stillman, "Academic Imperialism and Its Resolution: The Case of Economics and Anthropology," *American Scientist*, vol. 43 (1955), pp. 77–88.

horizon can hardly help including other territories than his own, even though he may assume that other people can't possibly understand his operation. Students in such a situation are often torn between their wish for a clear-cut departmental identity—one they would have no difficulty in explaining to themselves and to all comers—and the pressure on them against being discipline-bound and isolationist.

In less avant-garde institutions, however, I doubt if this pressure is very strong, while at the tail of the procession what is often lacking is any departmental or scholarly identity to speak of, as compared with the strength of ties to a particular college, or a particular denomination.[13] Indeed, colleges at or near the bottom, colleges which cannot afford the full line of departments, may be installing a course that combines psychology, group dynamics, cultural anthropology, and some elements of social work. Interdisciplinary courses as taught in under-privileged schools are often an avant-garde excuse for intellectual laxity and budgetary economy, but on the other hand in some impoverished schools the adoption of the model set at a leading institution has enabled them to overtake and surpass some of the middle range of colleges and universities still largely wedded to de-partmentalism, too well off to look for money-saving integrations, and too insecure to experiment.

---

[13] Strength of ties to a particular college is not always, of course, a sign of stagnation or lack of intellectual discipline. A number of colleges—Antioch, Reed, Amherst, Swarthmore, for example—that see themselves as models for the nation yet develop an intense devotion to the local institution and its total program. To some extent, this means that many who teach there are less eager than others of equal scholarly endowment to climb in the rank order of academia; they want to contribute to a college in addition to their contribution to a department which might, in theory, locate anywhere. (Research done by Alvin Gouldner, as yet unpublished, has helped me understand these pioneering forms of home-guard spirit.)

Professionalization and the Fear of the Layman

The insecurity at such places is understandable, for many of them have only just won from governing boards and legislatures acceptance of the standards set by accrediting agencies; they have done so by insisting scrupulously on the doctorate as a requirement for teaching and by obeying the severe model of the discipline set by the graduate schools from which their instructors are recruited (a phenomenon we discussed in the previous lecture as a factor in academic isomorphism). But, especially in a local climate of suspicion of the university, these victories are felt as precarious; there is always the fear that some regent or local businessman will ask: Why should the University of Nebraska, located in an agricultural state, offer so many esoteric courses, of no earthly use to good Nebraskans? Indeed, when I read the Chicago *Tribune,* I often feel that my own University exists in Illinois by the mere fiat of Mr. Rockefeller's money, that it is a planetary institution which should have extraterritorial rights! While in the previous lecture, I suggested, with an illustration drawn from the University of Buffalo Law School, that there might be advantages in regional specialization of institutions, I did not of course mean by that to imply that the customers' most parochial wants should be taken as mandates, without enlargement and redefinition. At any rate, universities in the middle range which have aimed to be more than corner service stations have frequently seen no other alternative than to appeal to the civic pride of their locale in doing as well as, or better than, some other academic point of reference.[14]

[14] I like to tell the story of the Kansas City matron whom I heard sigh with relief—"Thank goodness, that's over"—at the conclusion of a Philharmonic series: when I asked her why she attended the concerts, she replied: "Well, Dallas has a symphony orchestra, and so does St. Louis!"

However, precisely because this middle range of universities has tended to commit itself to literal-minded departmentalism, general education and interdisciplinary programs in that range may provide a rallying point for some of the less conventional men who are eager to cross departmental barriers—and who have ahead of them the discovery, implicit in what I am saying here, that when they have crossed one river there will be still other and wider ones, such as the very great gaps that at many institutions separate the natural from the social sciences, and the humanities from both. I hope they do not make that discovery only to be disillusioned, for what matters in teaching and intellectual work is not merely the product—the course program or the finding —but also the process: the ferment of discovery, the vocations cemented among students, the awareness of unexplored potentialities.

THE SCHOLAR'S COUNTRY

I have been talking about the boundaries which divide the disciplines from each other—and using "nationalism" or "isolationism" as metaphors. I want now to put these terms back into their usual context and to raise questions concerning the relation between a scholar's attachment to his field and to his country. I cannot here

---

In current talk about the shortage of math and science teachers, reference is constantly being made to the greater output of technicians in the Soviet Union. The reference is often made by people more interested in math than they are in the Cold War, and one trouble with employing such arguments, in which one's own motives are submerged, is that one never knows in the end whom they convince: each rhetorician may assume some other group requires these extrinsic and essentially Philistine and manipulative arguments and may end up by confusing himself— and if the Soviet Union should start training poets in place of metallurgists where would he be?

take up the whole problem of loyalty, but only examine the connection between recruitment into a discipline and emancipation from the ties of locality.

In an earlier day, before nationalism became as vehement a movement as it did in the nineteenth and twentieth centuries, the cosmopolitanism of the savant was part of a rather homogeneous international (though primarily Western) culture of the gentleman—a reminder of the Latinist culture of medieval clerks and, in the ease with which a man like Diderot could disregard territorial boundaries, an anticipation of today's international café society. Moreover, the climate of aristocracy (to which a man of humble and illegitimate birth such as Diderot could through talent gain entry) fostered the amateur spirit, with its distaste for the pedantic boundaries of the disciplines—an outlook still to be found among Oxford and Cambridge dons who seldom deign to talk shop and who cultivate a gentlemanly indifference to the race for priorities and preemption of fields. A versatile man like Jefferson, and those who modeled themselves on him, did not need to make a specialty of versatility—as now happens among those of us who move away from departmentalism towards integration.

Academic life today is democratic rather than aristocratic in tone, and scholars are made, not born. The altered pattern of recruitment could be expected to increase the proportion of nationalism, both of field and of country, in professorial attitudes—nationalism and democracy have, as we know from our own past and as we can see today in Africa and Asia, tended to be allies, and of course to spur mobility. There is some evidence (in studies made by Karl Deutsch at MIT) that scholars presently tend to cite foreign sources somewhat less than formerly (taking into account increases in domestic productivity), though one could also perhaps argue that

scholars in the West, along with other educated people,
are less crudely and vindictively nationalistic than they
were in the First World War. What we do find is that
American scholars, despite our country's tradition of
pluralism and of foreign study, are for the most part
readily enlisted in an era of total war and total loyalty;[15]
nationalism, among elites as among people in general,
remains a hardy perennial among evils and, perhaps,
when fierce and irresponsible new nations like Israel and
Pakistan get nuclear weapons, the finally catastrophic
evil.

Yet it is also true, as I have indicated, that a scholar's
loyalty to his field is the source of what Talcott Parsons
would call a certain universalizing quality in academic
life: a discipline can lift us out of our attachments to
home and mother, to our undergraduate alma mater, too,
and attach us instead to the new country of Biophysics

---

[15] I have found it sad in this connection that in the Oppenheimer hearings his defenders, such as Professor Smythe, apologized for what appeared to be Oppenheimer's lapses in total
obedience to security officers rather than trying to show that
Oppenheimer's complex and contextual moral code made him
a more responsible person than most of his detractors. The
transcript revealed Oppenheimer as a man courageous enough
to be more concerned with the fate of the planet than with
short-run placating of nationalists—he could guard the security of
this country in novel settings because he was less than wholly
preoccupied with protecting his own, or with compensating by
jingoism for earlier Party-line associations. Likewise, in the Peters
case, where he stressed to a secret House hearing Peters' Communist ties, and then sought in the Rochester press when the
news leaked to protect Peters' job at the non-classified University
of Rochester, he was not being two-faced (as his friends seemed
prepared to admit) but dealing with at least two conflicting
responsibilities: to national security and to international science
(also to humane sympathy even for Communists). Yet so difficult
is it to defend moral complexity in the simplified rhetoric of
public controversy that such items were taken by his friends
as conceded blots on his record rather than enhancements of it.
    In the next lecture, I shall recur to this problem of rhetoric
as it involves the schools; see pp. 132–135.

or the old of Medieval History. Reading Carl Becker's
essay "On Being a Professor" we can see how, via
Turner and the University of Wisconsin, he was pried
loose from the values of Black Hawk City, Iowa; he put
the matter with his customary grace: "Less than ever
did I desire to return to the known world and tread in
monotonous routine the dusty streets of Now and Here.
. . . How fine not to have 'to do' anything! And one
day it dawned upon me that this was precisely the case
of my admired professors. . . . From that moment I
was a lost man. I was bound to become a professor."[16]

In most countries, the academic profession is a career
open to talent (whatever the head start given one by
being born in the city rather than the country, or to a
family of at least modest means and driving standards
of achievement); and in the United States the relative
decline of ethnic and social-class snobberies and dis-
crimination, combined with the immense expansion of
the colleges, has drawn into scholarship a great majority
whose backgrounds are distinctly unscholarly.[17] Moreover, as the Knapp, Goodrich, and Greenbaum studies
reveal, a disproportionate number come from the small
liberal arts colleges of the Midwest. Knapp and Goodrich point out that students from small-town and rural
backgrounds who come from families of limited means
can find in an academic career a step up both in social-
class and occupational terms, and they suggest that the
advancing inner frontier of science has taken the place

[16] From *The Unpopular Review*, vol. 7 (1917), at pp. 344–
345. I owe the reference to Bernard Bailyn, and also the
suggestion that Becker's interest in climates of opinion was not
unrelated to his experience of changing intellectual atmospheres.

[17] See Logan Wilson's *The Academic Man: A Study in the
Sociology of a Profession* (New York: Oxford University Press,
1942) for similar findings. While sons of doctors often take up
medicine (and may have an inside track on getting into medical
school), sons of professors, like sons of ministers, frequently go
after a financially less constricting life.

for many of the frontier of the pioneers. They note also that many of the colleges where this transformation occurs are just emerging from Protestant denominational controls: the scientific vocation is a kind of one-step-up emancipation from previous theological concerns. It might be added to this that a student of limited horizons can find in his college professor an unanticipated model of a new way of life and of livelihood whereas the professor's life might seem bleak to a student of equal ability growing up in a large metropolis and attending a metropolitan university.

The Disciplinary Patriot

In this fashion, many of our intellectuals tend to be converts (what the Quakers call "convinced" Friends), not birthright adherents, with the immense seriousness of the convert and his need for justifications and rationalizations of his choice. For instance, Becker and Carper have shown, in studies of graduate students at the University of Illinois, how students who began by pursuing an M.D. and failed to get into medical school (sometimes because lacking in the proper background) end by obtaining a Ph.D. in physiology, calling medical men a bunch of guesswork operators, and confirming a new identity as research scientists. And whereas the practicing doctors on a medical faculty are by the nature of the case home-guard, attached to a particular class and clientele, the physiologists in the hospital are itinerants, attached to physiology.[18]

[18] See Howard S. Becker and James Carper, "The Development of Identification with an Occupation," *American Journal of Sociology*, vol. 61 (1956), pp. 289–298; and "The Elements of Identification with an Occupation," *American Sociological Review*, vol. 21 (1956), pp. 341–348. The authors observe that the philosophy students are strikingly unattached—philosophy is for them still a catch-all for the intellectual life as such, not another set of specialties.

Thus, as already implied, physiology has the capacity of engendering a non-territorial nationalism of its own. The fervency of this nationalism reflects the sacrifices the scholar has made to become a scholar, what he has had to surrender of earlier social-class origins and ambitions: physiology has to carry quite a freight when the parents of the physiologist have staked all on his becoming a doctor—a doctor of medicine and not the *ersatz* doctor of philosophy in a field they have never heard of, which moreover doesn't seem to bring either money or fame.

We can understand this process better by a brief comparison with European analogues. In France, for example, the student who has completed the lycée is regarded as a young adult, not as a member of a separate "youth culture," and when, as only rarely happens, he attends the university, he is incorporated into its ideological rather than its disciplinary divisions. If he joins the claque for a particular professor, it is more likely to be because of what the professor stands for (e.g., existentialism, or Merleau-Ponty-type Marxism) than because the professor's field has suddenly become the student's home away from home. The disciplines are not in any case news to the European student who has done what we would regard as college-level work at the lycée, Gymnasium, or public school. Furthermore, in attending the university he belongs (whether he likes the fact or not) to an elite, and his significant social-class differentiation minimizes his less salient disciplinary segregation—this is surely a factor in the easier amateurism of the British or Continental scholar in comparison with the American. (As democratization spreads, the European patterns are of course changing.) The American professor, in contrast to this, finds few colleagues among the mass of undergraduates on the basis either of a common culture or a common ideology in the political or eschatological sense. Instead, his techniques and methods of work, his implicit metaphysics of research, his nationalism of discipline or subdiscipline, his attacks on enemies in the department who do bad work and disgrace the field—these often rather ascetic bits and pieces make up the evangelism for recruiting an occasional student.

Anyone who thinks that vested interests are all economic knows nothing of intellectual life; investments in ideas, whether in the form of ideologies or of disciplines, involve what we have made of ourselves, and this is something no dean or chancellor, acting as mediator, can easily buy off.

THE DISCIPLINES AS "VETO GROUPS"

Implicit in all I have said is the notion that what my collaborators and I speak of in *The Lonely Crowd* as the "veto groups," the political and social blocs and groupings that frustrate political action in the United States, operate also in the intellectual realm, in terms of departments and fields. Each prevents the others from growing too big, from encompassing too much. While it takes tremendous energy and courage and vision to inaugurate a new field—consider, for example, James Breasted and the creation of Egyptology—the nationalistic investments of less courageous and less dogmatic men can serve to maintain an old field and even to give its development a certain autonomy.

This autonomy, which permits the discipline to transcend the motives and the problems which gave rise to it, has many positive sides, a point to which we shall return in a moment. But it also allows the discipline to act as a bloc in university politics to crush new potential disciplines which might threaten its control over funds or students; indeed, one reason for the strong presidential regimes which have characterized some American universities (as compared with control by colleagues at Oxford or Cambridge) has been the search for leverage against departmental self-protectiveness of this sort —of course, there are less exalted reasons also. Especially in the minds of timid students, the existing array of departments has a kind of Kantian *a priori* effect on the students' categories: they are the precoded forms of knowledge, and it is hard to learn to think in other codes. And although the foundations sometimes make brave efforts to establish new channels for distributing access to research funds, it is simpler all round if these flow through the existing departmental organization. Thus, each discipline is at the same time an institutionalization of the search for new knowledge and a barrier to that search.

When I have discussed these matters with Everett Hughes, he has stressed the realistic point that professors need the shell of a discipline with its comforts of colleagueship as an ever-available retreat. That is, he sees the labels of the disciplines as nominalist devices, behind which interdisciplinary effort goes on as individuals seek out collaborators and stimulators elsewhere. His argument is rather Burkean: once people have been initiated into a disciplinary tribe, they can then be free to wander with the passport that initiation gives them. His goal, if I understand him, is a series of covert coalitions, easily made, easily broken, rather than overt constitutions and covenants openly arrived at and dismayingly breached. He sees a license to specialize in any one field as a license to encourage a curiosity which takes little account of fields. By keeping open lines of renewal from and even retreat into the original field, he would hope to minimize "nativist" reactions.

This is all very well for the ensconced professor

who combines institutional protection with institutional know-how, but (as Jules Henry has emphasized in correspondence with me) it may not suffice for the students for whom the disciplinary barriers will appear impenetrable.[19] Students today—professors everywhere agree on this, irrespective of their own ideological perspective —are rarely rebellious; they accept the universe.[20] The existence of a wandering scholar here and there (whose colleagues may consider him a bit unsound) may not be enough to encourage students to tackle interdisciplinary topics themselves; they may need semantic support in the very organization of the university if they are to pursue the less clearly demarcated paths.

The Disciplines as Racecourses of the Mind

In these comments, I have been looking at the disciplines and their subdivisions as veto groups, stabilizing the market for ideas, policing it to some extent and thus controlling the worst charlatanry (as the Association of American Medical Colleges has so very effectively done for medical schools), and making large-scale reorgani-

[19] Let me make clear that, although my examples in these remarks are drawn from the major disciplinary divisions, such as economics or history, the same problems recur within these divisions, no matter how fine the sub-fields are sliced; the effort in each division to establish a core curriculum always reveals how many marginal specialties there are, and how difficult communication can be among them, though housed in the same departmental shell. Political science, for instance, is notable today for the gentlemanly warfare between old-style theorists and new-style behaviorists; that is, the "older" and the "newer" social science tendencies exist within, as much as among, the principal disciplines, and most established disciplines are loose and often accidental aggregations of topic, tradition, and method, in search of a common rationale.

[20] There are, as one might expect, a few colleges way down in the academic procession where students have become more alert than heretofore—fundamentalist-controlled colleges, for example, to which the "newer" social sciences are just beginning to spread.

zations of large-scale universities almost as difficult as comparable reorganizations in the political realm. I have postponed full attention to some of the advantages of organizing scholarship after this fashion.

If we look at a field from the inside, we can see that it embraces a series of intellectual tracks down which we run, protected by our lines from having to look in too many directions at once, and able to hand on the torch to another runner on the same track. Indeed, if we think about the sport of running on an actual track, it seems a crazy thing to do, which only Greek Olympians and modern schoolboys and collegians would dream of. It appears terribly remote from life—yet it somehow represents it, recreates it, and even adds to its quality and complexity. The same is true on the track of a discipline; looked at from the perspective of our national problems, it also seems remote and crazy like a sport, and it so strikes perhaps the majority of students. But the discipline is a protection against looking to the students as the sole audience of our performance, and we always hope that if we run well enough, some students will join the race too, and become as crazy as we.

Any approach to a subject in terms exclusively of what we choose to call "real life," no matter how stimulating pedagogically, will almost inevitably mislead the student as to the "real life" of the disciplines themselves—a life built on virtuosity of concepts, on abstractions and models, and of course on pedantry as well. Just as institutional economics, which deals with the auto industry or the garment industry or labor relations, doesn't seem to the analytical economist to be economics at all but rather a backward sociology of a particular clientele, so to the general psychologist or generalizing sociologist anything so specific as a particular person or relation does not seem to be true psychology or sociology. The clinician is as much excluded in the one case as in the other. Life can only enter a discipline under the aegis of a label, that is, of a generalization or a theory.

The Problem of Intellectual Commitment

Yet, as we all know, any single discipline tends to leave too much out, or just as often to leave too much in without knowing that it is there. The older, that is, the less-social social sciences, took their theories of human nature and culture for granted. In wide circles, they succeeded in indoctrinating politicians and the public with their more or less rationalist vocabulary: we learned to talk easily about interest groups, about power, about the flow of goods and credit, about constitutional and legal matters, that once were recondite. Then came the profound shock of discovering political and economic irrationality—of finding that the mass movements of totalitarianism did not seem to fit a nineteenth-century vocabulary. People looked about for a vocabulary less colored by its very applicability to a particular epoch and its institutions, and they felt that the language of the newer social sciences was somehow less committed, and could therefore grapple with the puzzles presented by men who voted and selected their buys against reason, against interest. All language is of course loaded, but the loadings of psychological and sociological terms were unfamiliar—as were the events themselves. The traditional disciplines appeared to block understanding by their very clarity. At the same time that the genius of Freud offered the possibility of new interpretations, his complex pessimism also appeared attractive, and his system, like that of the economists, was a self-sealing one. Thus, a number of gifted people, trained in the older fields, looked for guidance to the new fields—men such as Harold D. Lasswell and

Judge Jerome Frank. At some schools, men of this stamp have succeeded in giving the old fields a new look.

And yet one of the obvious, if paradoxical, advantages of nationalism and parochialism is to prevent all fields from becoming alike, or even influencing each other too much. (This is one attraction to romanticists about the class structure of feudalism.) There is even an advantage, in certain contexts, of permitting the disciplines to go on leaving things out which should be taken account of. For there is a prevalent attitude—it might be called the democratization of theories—which insists that all factors, for a factor comes from a theory, must be taken into account, must be given a vote and a voice; to stress some things more than others is "undemocratic," even *unfair* to the intellectual veto groups that have a right to lobby for their factors.[21] That is, these "groups" operate in the very structure of our ideas, where each set of factors acts as it were as a counterpoise to other sets of factors, and all risk of intellectual action and commitment is avoided.

Creativity and Coercion

The history of the psychoanalytic movement provides as good an example as any. In Freud's hands, psychoanalysis sought (like Marxism and even more like Leninism) rapid closure: it left out of account a great deal—cultural factors, cognitive ones, humanistic ones. Yet it is striking that Alfred Adler, who put many of these things back in, has had a very limited impact in comparison with Freud's, for (as Erich Fromm has pointed out in lectures) Adler purchased common sense at the price of loss of imaginative sharpness. Freud was attractive precisely because he had something of Nietzsche's

21 For further discussion of this theme, see note 22, p. 165 *infra*.

ferocity and even solipsism—because his system high-lighted certain previously neglected things and aggres-sively omitted others. Common sense is codified and therefore partly falsified reality; Freud showed us a way out of it. Thereafter, his work often served to create the very evidence of its own limitations (as when an-thropologists looked for the Oedipus complex in the Trobriands and elsewhere), and what was missing is being rapidly incorporated in our psychocultural theories.

I cannot tell you how many research proposals I have read which declare that the topic—whether it be men-tal health, race relations, or productivity—will be ap-proached "from all points of view"—including the phys-iological. The history of science does not support the notion that the way to make progress is to be eclectic and leave nothing out. In my opinion, commitment is more important than inclusiveness both in teaching and research, provided that the commitment is not merely an inherited one. To be concrete, I have been involved with several research projects where it has been pro-posed that we "bring in a psychologist." I have opposed this, while recognizing that there are aspects to our prob-lem which, without a psychologist, we shall miss. It will be time enough, after our work is published, for the psychologists to correct us for these oversights, but if we begin by trying to be just to all standpoints we shall lack the courage to be mistaken, the courage to stress something too much.

These are matters about which we could use a great deal more knowledge, for all too little is known about the conditions for creativity, about the balances of strangeness and at-homeness men need if they are to be productive. What has to be fought is complacency. But complacency may sometimes appear in following a nar-row and comfortable track laid out by one's departmental teachers, and at other times in giving each intellectual vector one vote to keep it quiet. There is no escape from the scholar's own risky decision as to what is more important and what is less important. Often, his apparently generous feeling that nothing should be left out rests on fear that *he* will be left out—that is, that he will be found to have neglected some important factor. Thus, he plays it safe, leaves room for everything—for geographic influences and economic ones, for psychological and sociological, historical and teleological, so that no one can accuse him of leaving any influence unrepresented. Yet we know, if we look at the results of the work of Marx or Darwin,[22] Turner or Boas, Max Weber or Clark Hull, that science thrives on sins of omission, and on putting back what has been thrown out.

Please remember that I am talking about leaving out *factors*, i.e., approaches and conceptual schemes, and not about leaving out *facts*. The best theories embrace as many facts as they can hold at once, and there is usually more danger from ignoring apparently trivial and underprivileged facts than from trying to attend to them. Yet even there one can become too permissive, too "democratic" as it were. It is obvious that at some point, both in course construction and research design, one has to stop one's ears to the facts, and take one's chances with the facts one has.

[22] Robert Redfield has some thoughtful things to say concerning Darwin's quarter-century of conversation with himself before publishing *The Origin of Species*. See *The Educational Experience* (Pasadena: The Fund for Adult Education, 1955), pp. 29–31. Intellectual "lead-times" like those of Darwin seem to me very rare today, at least in the sciences.

TREND-THINKING AND AUTONOMY

Let me stress, in this connection, a general caution about the tenor of my remarks in these lectures. I have been talking about trends, and about the dialectic of advance and defeat, progress and despair, which occurs in intellectual as in other institutions. These things like other topics in the sociology of knowledge are, I believe, interesting; it can be useful and even important to understand these trends—useful, for one thing, so that one doesn't blame oneself or one's colleagues or the dean for difficulties inherent in the cultural setting. And yet, on another level, it would be a terrible surrender of initiative for individual students and scholars to be overinfluenced by trends. To allow one's curiosities to be swayed by market research is like allowing vocational guidance and aptitude tests to determine one's career—such tests may help placate a parent who is pressuring one, or help clarify the sources of talent or blockage of talent, but they can never properly direct us: choice, while not unrelated to aptitude, should not be subservient to it. The revival of classical studies at a few institutions would never have happened if scholars had individually believed what they collectively "knew," namely that the classics were doomed. Since we do have a full-employment society, we can afford, indeed require, many activities which might appear wasteful to a cosmic planner of the intellectual division of labor, and there seems to be no necessity for scholars to sacrifice their own bent and curiosity because the market quotation for their discipline is falling. This is especially so since, as I indicated in my first lecture, many academics already follow the Dow-Jones averages and will be riding whatever trends appear.

I also want to make clear that I do not put myself

above the tendencies I am describing, nor do I consider
myself superior to intellectual fashion, simply because
I believe in countering it. As Georg Simmel observed,
he who goes counter to the mode is also a victim of
modishness. I have myself, as many of you know,
switched from the older social sciences, having studied
law and government, to the newer ones, and while I
have not abandoned my interest in the larger political
questions, I have recently approached them with the
roundabout methods of social psychology. Furthermore,
I have suffered in research enterprises from the over-
ambitious claims of these newer sciences of which I have
been part. The claims are in some measure a humane
response to evident societal needs, including needs for
understanding, but they are also in part an effort of
restless men to justify a line of goods. This effort gets us
involved in a series of institutional and personal research commitments in which the success of each project is necessary less in its own intrinsic terms than as
part of an institutional strategy of inter- and intra-
academic competition of the sort I described in my first
lecture. In this way, the fate of colleagues gets bound
up with the fate of an idea or a method. This has always
been true of social movements, but only in recent years
has social research become a movement as elaborate as
all that. It takes greater strength of will and clarity of
judgment than most people—including myself—have
had to escape these ambiguities and the loss of independence.

A small-town boy who goes to college may be lifted
by that encounter into the wild blue yonder of the
mind: a discipline, with its national and even international market of ideas, can free him from the ethnocentric nest of home and parish, give him a new past (the
traditions of "his" field) and a new identity. The college

he attends escapes by similar devices the rigidities of the community in which—as it appears to many of the faculty—it merely happens to be located; its national connections, e.g., in the AAUP, give it a modicum of protection against the anti-scientific venom of many of the half-educated in America (it is of course also protected by the misunderstanding of its emancipating functions, screened as these may be by athletics, fraternities, and other "collegiate" doings). Intellectual mobility is highly correlated with other forms of movement, such as the social and occupational mobility which W. Lloyd Warner and his collaborators have studied; and the American scholar is likely to be one step in the class system above his family origins, with the wider orbits the upper-middle class provides;[23] moreover, we have seen in the first lecture that the colleges themselves are on the move—and that the "newer" social sciences are among the fastest escalators.

Yet we have also seen that the emancipation achieved by these disciplinary attachments turns out to possess its own built-in "governors." Graduate school for many begins a training in constraint and constriction—so much so that too often I have seen undergraduate students whom I knew as bold and bright become scared and unimaginative—sometimes actually rather stupid—as

[23] This development is itself one important justification for academic expansion, along with the expansion of other cultural and intellectual activities in a society whose work-force is steadily moving out of the extractive and manufacturing occupations. It is true that many social scientists and novelists agree that entering the professional middle class is entering the arena of constraint, not of variety; this is an aspect of their fond view of the more casual aggression, relaxation, and sexuality in the lower class. In any event, for reasons partly to be dealt with in my next lecture, the lower-class privileges appear to be spreading upwards in the class system, even while middle-class privileges spread downwards. Valuing choice and variety as sources of good in spite of confusion and anxiety, it seems to me that the liberation in entering the middle class ordinarily outweighs the suffering.

they went on in graduate work. The disciplines at the graduate level often turn out to be new parishes with impalpable and amorphous—hence anxiety-producing—boundaries; these protect one at once against old prejudices and new facts. Scholars who enter a field because of what it can do for them in career terms (rather than because of what they can do for it) often end up as members of intellectual blocs—gatekeepers insisting on tolls being paid to their fields and their preferred factors from any intellectual traffic.

Involved in all these developments are the not always fortunate consequences of democracy and equalitarianism in intellectual life—consequences in the nationalistic vehemence of the *arrivistes* on the one hand, and the loss of aristocratic defenses for scientific skepticism on the other hand. Yet democracy has also meant that, as we have seen, intellectual and academic careers have been opened to many thousands who would otherwise have been forced by circumstance to remain parochial—and reverential to their "betters." The combined energies of these men have pushed knowledge forward in this country with an energy akin to that of business expansion; new fields have been opened and staked out; and universities have moved rapidly to assimilate avant-garde innovations in specialization and in integration. The burgeoning market that results also provides a certain freedom for the professor who has disciplinary and cosmopolitan as well as local contacts, for he can exercise a personal veto power over academic autocracy by going somewhere else—a power that forces college presidents to compete for talent by filling in their organization chart with the chiaroscuro of public relations. But the freedom that permits a particular man to escape from a particular oppression—and to join with others in the AAUP and elsewhere to fight more generalized oppression—has of course its limits. A "controversial" man may have no place at all to go: even the whole country may for him be but a glorified parish, unless he is lucky enough to find a college which at that moment wants to prove something by taking him on (a controversial group, such as the one that waged the California Oath fight); the braver places will keep such a man if they already are committed to him, but will seldom invite trouble by taking him on *de novo*.

To be sure, no law provides that universities should be responsible for all of high culture, though we have come in recent years pretty close to accepting the academic life as the nearly universal vehicle for intellectual pursuits and even artistic ones. It is rather that professors seem to feel that without their disciplines and their colleges they would be lost (apart from realistic problems of teamwork and research equipment); as many have pointed out, the "free intellectual" of Karl Mannheim's writings, institutionally uncommitted, is today a rarity. As we cast up these gains and losses, we realize once more that no victory of liberation is ever final.

III

SECONDARY EDUCATION

AND "COUNTER-CYCLICAL"

POLICY

In my last lecture, I talked about some of the ways in which the world of the colleges, and of particular fields within them, especially the newer social sciences, is a national one, limited here and there by home-guard concerns but on the whole transcending parish boundaries. True, we have seen that some of the smaller colleges are despotically run, and that the professors are treated, not as independent professionals bound by the standards of their discipline, but as hired hands in a business more autocratic than many businesses are today. Indeed, as suggested in my previous lecture, one major problem of academic freedom is how to strengthen the spine of the college teacher who lacks independent means, colleaguial support, or connections beyond his present college, and thus lacks even a limited veto power over trustee or presidential absolutism. In theory, academics form a guild all of whom treat each other as equals; but to belong to the guild effectively one needs the power to leave any particular college whose patterns are authoritarian or, for other reasons, oppressive. And for this the market for college teachers is, despite the coming explosion in enrollments, not quite sufficiently free, not quite sufficiently elastic. Therefore, many college teachers are worse off in terms of job security than school teachers with a strong union in a large city system— worse off, too, because their title of professor may lead them to expect more autonomy than they dare fight for.

Over all, however, there is no doubt that the colleges are much freer than the high schools; as we have seen, by calling something a college, one enters another league, another set of constituencies. It is a league, moreover, in which the publicly controlled institutions benefit from the high standards of academic courage and freedom set at pace-maker private colleges, such as Harvard, MIT, Sarah Lawrence, Chicago, which have fought back against Senator McCarthy and other professional heresy-hunters, while refusing to placate reactionaries among their own alumni.[1] By contrast, at the high school level there is no comparable private model: the public school is the dominant institution in secondary education—in fact, the only one that comes to mind in many parts of the country.

THE SECONDARY SCHOOL'S VULNERABILITY IN THE COMMUNITY

However, it is obvious that not all secondary school systems are alike: they differ as much among themselves

[1] This, of course, is not intended to deny the fact that Wisconsin, Minnesota, and (in some measure) California have as proud traditions of freedom as the leading private universities; even so, they profit as do other public institutions from the responsibility the latter have felt for the nationwide climate of freedom—a reponsibility understood by their leading trustees and administrators.

as the colleges do. A few big-city and suburban public
high schools (such as Boston Latin, Winnetka's New
Trier, the Scarsdale schools, New York City's High
School of Music and Art or Stuyvesant High, etc.) have
quite as much of a tradition of intellectual distinction
and even as devoted and protective alumni as all but a
small handful of private schools—and offer a far better
education than many colleges do. Occasionally, as happened in Pasadena, such schools may lose a fight for
freedom and experimentalism, but they recognize the
fight as theirs.

Apart from such outstanding exceptions, the high
schools are today in many ways in the position the colleges were a hundred years ago. In their need to monitor
idly prankish youth, in their collegiate razzle-dazzle of
sports and dating, in their fear of being called "godless," in their need (not financial but political) to accept whoever comes, in their unavoidable concern with
morals, they recall many vignettes we have of nineteenth-century college life. Of course, the differences are
great, too: the high schools today involve the whole
community in a way that even the colleges with the
most vociferous subway alumni neither did nor do; and
one could argue that in some ways high school youth is
presently more mature and more sober than college
youth of the collegiate generations. Moreover, when we
read W. Lloyd Warner's *Democracy in Jonesville* and
August B. Hollingshead's description of the same Midwest small town in *Elmtown's Youth*, we are reminded
of still another feature of the early American college,
namely, its emphasis on parental social standing as the
basis for seating and even for honors; for these books
show the high school and its teachers to be almost completely dominated by the "better element," to the extent of influencing grades given and such honors as leading the band, according to the social-class position of

the family. The same theme of class (and in the South, caste) domination of the schools appears in other books of the Warner group, such as Allison Davis' and John Dollard's *Children of Bondage*, and in John Gillin's chapter on "The School in the Context of the Community" in *Education and Anthropology*.

Which Public Runs the Schools?

Other studies, however, have shown rapid democratizing tendencies to be at work in the control of the schools just as these tendencies have also, in hardly more than a generation, altered the high school from a college preparatory institution for one-fifth or so of the teen-agers (or an occasional terminal institution for the girls) to the taken-for-granted pattern for four-fifths or more. In a number of communities the school boards have become highly democratic in the sense of reflecting, with at least equal voice, the less educated and the less privileged strata. Thus, in one New England manufacturing city, the superintendency and the school board have become the symbols, even more than such an office as the mayoralty, of ethnic and class conflict, with the Irish and to a lesser degree the French Canadians getting their revenge on the Beacon Hill-type snobs of earlier generations. Since the lower-class parent has no interest in the schools, save as a political symbol, unless his own children are of school age, this means that the superintendent of schools must, if he lasts that long, educate a new group of constituents every few years—a totally different situation from that of the private school headmaster who has managed to cultivate a self-perpetuating body of trustees.[2]

[2] I am indebted for materials on the politics of the "Bay City" schools to as yet unpublished memoranda by James Shipton and Peter and Alice Rossi. Another study, done by Neal Gross, Ward

Likewise, an unpublished study done on the West Coast has shown how the school board in an expanding industrial town became the most representative agency in the town, speaking not only for the newcomer industrialists but for the farmers and others of lesser education who didn't want to see any "new-fangled notions" in the schools, any more than they wanted to see the town's water monkeyed with by fluoridation—this last being, as I mentioned in my second lecture, an issue on which the more parochial have in some towns mobilized to defeat the more cosmopolitan and science-minded higher status groups.

The handful of studies we have (including the Lynds' close scrutiny of the control of the "Middletown" schools) do not, of course, cover the entire area or even allow us readily to interpret the data we already have; thus, we know that Middletown and Elmtown are (or were) to some degree company towns and possibly not representative of their regions. We do know that there are schools so located as to be able to profit from a balance of powers in the community—that is, to be powers themselves, able to give a cagey and purposeful superintendent quite a free hand within very broad limits—so long at least as no dramatic issue presents a group in the community with a chance to make trouble for him and capture votes and symbolic vindications for itself. Indeed, the teachers themselves, in alliance with school board members, have been known to drive a superintendent out, though on the whole they tend to stay out of fights at the hierarchy's peak and, like the consci-

Mason, and their colleagues at the Harvard School of Education, includes case studies of the role of New England school superintendents in coping with a wide variety of publics, including their teachers. The pressures to which they respond, moreover, are not merely local. For educators, despite what some of their university critics say, can read, and are not unaffected by the philosophies of education that emanate from the cultural and scientific centers.

entious civil servants they often are, to fall into line
with any workable mandate from "downtown."

In rural areas, matters are again different. Warren
Peterson found, in his study of women high school
teachers in Kansas City, that many had entered the Kansas City system after sad experiences of rural and small-
town politics, where a single shift in the school board
might eliminate a school principal and virtually dispos-
sess his teachers; in comparison, a metropolitan school
system offered the security of tenure, often enforced by
a union, as well as greater opportunity to specialize.

Altered Patterns of Pressure on the Teacher

The harassment of the public school teacher has been
traditional in the smaller American communities, but
this used to take the form (particularly if the teacher
was a woman) of policing her private life, her smoking
and gallivanting and church-going, without much direct
interference in her conduct of the classroom. Today,
especially in the larger places, the teacher is much
freer to lead her own private life, but what we might
term her academic freedom is under a great deal of
pressure. Lack of concern over the teacher's private
life reflects the general urbanization of America and the
decline of puritanical vigilance over teachers, ministers,
and other exemplars; meanwhile, however, concern over
the teacher as a person has taken on a new aspect; the
teacher is required today to be a "good guy," warm and
friendly, not too eccentrically dedicated to interests in
which the community cannot share. Moreover, the personality of the teacher has become more closely inter-
twined with the subjects taught: the high schools, which
could remain fairly remote from immediate community
preoccupations when attended only by a few, are now
under a service-minded pressure to teach the social

studies, and in many places they are also under pressure to teach a kind of syncretistic and neutral religion, as well as to teach tolerance, democracy and citizenship, and all other good things.[3]

Teaching these topics, which contain more obvious dynamite than the limited traditional curriculum did, however, both draws on what is in the papers and risks getting into them. High school teachers can become labeled by their students as "controversial" as soon as any discussion in the social area gets at all heated or comes close to home.[4] While a college student usually has to take the trouble to write home before he can get a parent steamed up about what a teacher has said in class, and in fact is quite likely to protect his teacher against his less enlightened parents, the secondary school student is still living at home with parents whose jealousy of the teacher is not mediated by distance either of space or of status. The high school teacher has in fact lost relative status in recent years as more and more parents are themselves high school graduates. And while the kindergarten teacher gains admiration because she can control several dozen preliterates whose mothers cannot always manage even one, the high school social studies teacher has a harder time being one-up on American-

[3] In smaller communities, as Wilbur Brookover points out in *The Sociology of Education*, the high schools also have in the past borne much of the obligation to furnish entertainment—through sports, debates, plays, music, etc.—a function from which the mass media, the country clubs, and do-it-yourself are gradually relieving them.

[4] A number of investigations have asked high school students what they consider as the qualities of a good teacher; this "consumer research" indicates a preference for clear explanations, good discipline and impartiality (no pets), good grooming, consideration for pupils' feelings, patience and kindness. These are hardly the qualities easiest for the dedicated social science teacher to cultivate! See, e.g., Sister M. Theophane and Arlene Rasor, "Good Teaching as Seen by Junior High School Pupils," *School Review*, vol. 54 (1956), pp. 72–75.

born parents who can claim to know as much as she
about civics or UNESCO.

THE SOCIAL STUDIES AS A CASE IN POINT

Considering this situation in an essay a few years ago,
I proposed that social studies be abandoned in the public schools, since they could not, without more protection for the teachers, be taught with any vigor or candor;
I argued that without this they were apt to become
sheer piety or, as they are called in one school, the "social slops." Rather than having the teachers assign news-
magazines and deal with current debates, or try to show
that the Brazilians or even the Chinese are human, too,
and live in an interesting way, I suggested they stick to
languages, mathematics, and the arts. These are disciplines that can be taught without political compromise
(other than that of allowing poor students to pass),
and they can be adequately, if sometimes crushingly,
taught by a person who is neither courageous nor
inspiring.[5]

---

[5] My article, "Some Observations on Intellectual Freedom,"
appeared in The American Scholar, vol. 23 (1954), pp. 9–25,
and is reprinted in Individualism Reconsidered and Other Essays,
pp. 123–138.
    Patrick Hazard has in correspondence made a point I fully
agree with, namely that the arts can, if illuminatingly taught, be
quite as controversial—even as "political"—as the social sciences,
but for most teachers, regrettably, the invitation to controversy is
a latent one in the arts and an unavoidable one in the social
studies. I am also aware that teachers of such allegedly non-contro-
versial subjects as French and algebra, basketball and shop, do
often manage to convey social attitudes all the more effectively
by pretending not to—convey them by side-comments or even by
the way they conduct themselves in class; it would often be well
to have such unexamined attitudes clarified and counterposed by
social studies teachers who make explicit their preference for
detached factuality as against side-of-the-mouth indoctrination.

John Dewey, with his orientation towards problem-solving as the principal basis of thought, and towards the school as a factor in the life of the community, would probably have regarded my view as an unwarranted concession to reaction. He might have pointed out, as many of my critics did, that even today perhaps no more than a third of our high school students go on to college, and the rest, were social studies abandoned, would get no formal orientation in a confusing world. And, just because the social studies do connect, if not taught too badly, with contemporary themes, they may occasionally help the teacher make contact with students for whom the traditional curriculum seems meaningless and remote—students who would otherwise drop out of school or, what is worse, remain physically present while learning how to evade the school's requirements—thus, in effect preparing themselves to do the same in the jobs they will hold later on.

"Facts" versus "Values"

My attitude on this matter has also been influenced by a chain of reflections set off by Max Weber's influential argument that the social scientists must eschew values in doing their work (although not in selecting a topic), and must in that sense separate their work from their personal lives and their unarguable preferences. It struck me that Weber's position was an understandable one for a German professor who feared among his colleagues and students the development at the close of the First World War of a romantic anti-democratic movement; he wanted to caution them that the world of the future required of them a stoical factuality, a rational appraisal of the new situation rather than a self-indulgent reaction against it. Today, among many in the avant-garde universities of this country, such a position is no longer progressive, and social science teachers who confront uncommitted, city-wise students who wouldn't dream of fighting city hall are often likely to emphasize the role of values in research and to attempt to smoke out the evasions and self-deceptions of empiricism.[6] But in many Southern or denominational colleges the situation is in this country today very much like that which Weber faced forty years ago: in these relatively unemancipated places youngsters arrive crammed full of values —their parents' and townsfolk's—but very shy on facts; and it is obviously an achievement to bring some detachment into their perspective, some sublimation of naïve, often chivalric vehemence. At the same time, by stressing his hard factuality, a college teacher in such a setting may escape censure, at least outside of the areas of greatest passion such as race relations or Communism, where presentation even of facts, no matter how judiciously, may be regarded as subversive.

The same possibility is open to the high school social studies teacher, who may present a model of dispassionateness to students still deeply imbued with the unthought-out values they grew up with, or the sometimes more frivolous opinions they have picked up from the peer-group or the media. Such an approach has its obvious dangers, first in not safeguarding the teacher or the students from community vigilantes, and second in its relative narrowness of range, for there will be some students in almost every school who would profit from seeing the way an informed and conscientious teacher himself decides "loaded" questions rather than simply "giving both sides." While such complexity can more readily be handled in college than in the secondary schools, we are still a long way from sending every stu-

[6] For fuller discussion, cf. my article (written in collaboration with Nathan Glazer), "Some Observations on Social Science Research," in *Individualism Reconsidered*, pp. 467–483.

dent to college, or even every bright student. Thus, it is likely that the social studies teacher can be emancipating for many of his students even if the best he can do is to introduce a bit of data and a bit of respect for it.

Can We Leave It to the "Documentary" Media?

I did, however, assume when I wrote my criticism of high school social studies that such introduction did not need to be made within the confines of the school, and that the high school students would be exposed to many of the themes of the social studies outside of school, particularly through the mass media. Radio and TV are censored, too, as the schools are, but the veto groups which affect them, being national in scope, are sometimes less parochial than the vested interests which can curb a public school teacher—or indeed see to it that there is nothing to curb. Many of the enthusiasts for educational TV, including myself, have hoped to provide intellectual challenge for young people through a still-young medium, not bound by tradition or tied to the school boards. In sober moments, however, I realize that countervailing power must be sought within, as well as outside, the schools. If teachers cannot occasionally make contact with a student's mind, the teachers will be dead on their feet and the young in their care will be stultified, no matter what programs "Omnibus" puts on. The school teacher may lack prestige in the eyes of the community at large, but the school as an institution has an unavoidable impact on the child—an impact almost as great as that of his parents. This is of course not an argument against experimentation with the media.[7] Perhaps a TV program can be, for a share-

[7] A promising approach seeks to link the schools to the media by class discussion of popular culture figures such as Milton Berle and Marlon Brando. In pre-television days, Reuel Denney, when he was an English teacher at Technical High in Buffalo, sought

our Black Metropolises, something of the catalyst that
pulp fiction was for Richard Wright (as he describes his
grim upbringing in *Black Boy*), namely, an escape from
the all-too-omnipresent "reality" into another world of
fantasy and imagination. But at present we know that
most such children will find what is vacuous in the
media to confirm their street and school experience,
rather than to prevail against it.

---

to come to meaningful terms with vocationally oriented boys by
alternating discussions of the rhetoric of comic strips or Fred Allen
with the required work in Shakespeare and Milton. More recently,
scattered experimenters have coalesced into the beginnings of a
movement. Marshall McLuhan of the University of Toronto has
been arguing that the contemporary media are restoring the
imagery and color that Gutenberg got rid of, and Patrick Hazard
has been writing regularly in *Scholastic*, *The Clearing House*,
and other periodicals read by secondary school teachers, concerning
the problems of using TV programs, popular music, and like
products as systematic grist for critical class discussion.

I am, it goes without saying, willing to defend these adventures
against the current scourge of academic demagogues who see
in any such development a soft Deweyite departure from tradition
—much as Senator Kefauver pretends to find in comic books
the source of juvenile delinquency. Nevertheless, I have my own
misgivings as I envisage school teachers whose training has given
them only the shadow of a connection with any literary and
humanistic tradition chatting with their classes about George
Gobel or the latest feuds in the Arthur Godfrey household
of professional pets. McLuhan, Hazard, Alan M. Thomas of
Teachers College, and some members of the College English
Association who have been working in the same direction bring
standards gained from Flaubert and Blackmur (and understanding
based on such social science works as W. Lloyd Warner and
William E. Henry or Herta Herzog on soap opera appeals) to
bear on Gobel and Godfrey, but as we saw in my first lecture,
professors in the teachers colleges seldom possess such wide
horizons—and might simply discover a new rationalization allowing
their students to justify the thirty hours a week they may already
spend with television.

No Road Back

All these considerations have brought me around to conceding that there is no presently viable alternative to some high school social studies programs—quite apart from the moral and practical problem of abandoning a program, for whatever good reasons, at the same time that it is under attack from conservatives who want to go back to the old-fashioned curriculum and from reactionaries who want the social studies revamped to drill the students in their version of Americanism. For those who are going on to college, the social studies might well be postponed, but for those who are not—and they cannot simply be consigned to vocational courses—the high schools have perforce become an *ersatz* college with all that implies in curricular and extra-curricular patterning. Nevertheless, I cannot comfortably resign myself to a dilemma in which teachers are forced, in a setting far less protected than that even of relatively unfree colleges, to take positions (including text adoptions) that may get them into trouble with vigilante groups on the one side or their own consciences on the other. Some school teachers have felt I was patronizing them in discouraging courageous behavior on their part, but of course I have nothing but praise for those who willingly take the risks involved in intrepid social studies teaching. But no school system can count on possessing even a minority of such teachers—for perhaps the majority, in fact, the dilemmas I have been discussing will scarcely exist, so encapsulated are they in the uncriticized values of their local communities.

Fighting Fire with Water

The schools' vulnerability is in part a matter of the

rhetoric of community controversy. Suppose, as now often happens, a demand is made for religious instruction
in the schools. The superintendent or school principal
is against this: he thinks it can only be mushy, not truly
religious—that, if anything, it will turn the kids against
religion and against each other. To explain all this
would take time and require some sophistication among
the parents and in the press, while his critics will label
him as "godless" if he resists. Or, to take another instance, there was a typical letter a short while ago
(March 12, 1956, by Nancy McGannon) in the Chicago *Daily News* attacking the President of a division
of the Illinois Education Association for resisting one of
the Broyles Bills requiring all teachers to take a loyalty
oath; the writer said she couldn't understand how academic freedom was abridged by such legislation and
ended by declaring: "I'm afraid there are a lot of parents
and taxpayers who do not understand it." It is hard to
imagine this "parent and taxpayer" writing a similar letter about her inability to grasp the import of one of the
Hoover Commission reports or the Report of the President's Council of Economic Advisers, yet the "parents
and taxpayers" do suppose that they can advise on matters having to do with education. When the President
of the Illinois Education Association sought to answer
her, the reply took nine paragraphs; it spelled out the
ambiguity of requiring a special test oath of teachers,
while at the same time it met the parent on the common
ground of patriotism and anti-Communism. The very
fact that the more complex positions take longer to state
puts the teacher on the defensive to start with, for at
best the teacher's position will be given equal chrono-
logical time and that will not suffice for clarification
(unless she has the rare ingenuity for putting complex
matters simply). The closer a word is to a blow, the
greater its impact in the short run and the harm is done;

in many controversies over the schools, there is no long run, little distance between the partisans, and few constitutional barriers to impetuosity.

Power of the Press

One important barrier, however, is implicit in what has already been said, namely, a liberal and enterprising press (broadcasting, because of its lack of permanence and its usual political irrelevance or neutrality, usually matters less). A vigorous press—even a good student paper—can act as a counter-cyclical force in its own right, and alter the patterns of public rhetoric in favor of the more complex as against the mindless. I have been repeatedly struck with the influence of the local papers on the climate of freedom or miasma at particular universities. A few colleges are so secure as not to be hurt or helped by the press (for instance, Harvard's Corporation and Overseers would in any case be more influenced by the *Herald-Tribune* than by the Boston *Post* or Hearst papers); and many are so benighted as not to learn from any source that freedom is as necessary to a college as a library or stadium. But when I compare in the Middle West the free state universities with the beleaguered ones, it seems to me that Wisconsin professors profit by reading Evjue's *Capital Times* (or the liberal Milwaukee paper) as breakfast-table reminders of support—profit, too, from knowing that waverers might even be intimidated from going against the current. Minnesota profits (as does Iowa) from the open-minded Cowles press in much the same way. By contrast, professors at Ohio State pick up the Columbus *Dispatch* anxiously, worrying what it might imply to other professors, and the administration, about how Senator Bricker, or some other regent, feels about their last speeches or books or even classroom comments. The reactionary professors feel heartened by the paper to vent their venom on the liberals; waverers get confused. Plainly enough, if a professor were sure neither administration nor regents nor state legislators pay the slightest attention to the paper, he would view its attacks as a joking matter rather than as a nightmare. However, it is sometimes hard to know which comes first: for a liberal press, as at Madison, may be as much the result as the cause of a free spirit among the faculty.

THE TWILIGHT CASE OF THE JUNIOR COLLEGE

In spite of what I have just said about the occasionally large or even disproportionate influence of the local paper on a university, it remains true that the colleges, including those which are publicly controlled, are much less within the purview of the parish than are the high schools. There are intermediate cases which illuminate this difference, and I was recently involved in one of them. It was the sort of subterranean academic freedom case that is common today, where the individual faculty man seeks to avoid national publicity, though it might vindicate him, lest it also make it harder for him to get another job while in addition embarrassing colleagues and superiors who are men of good will but are not exactly spoiling for a fight. The man in question, a sociologist, had been given a contract to teach in a junior college controlled by a large metropolitan school system, but before he could begin, police and FBI reports on his alleged radical past reached headquarters and his contract was revoked. In discussing the case with headquarters people, Everett Hughes and I found a great concern lest harm unjustly befall the instructor— the concern one might find in a decent paternalistic business—but virtually no realization that any principle was at stake, any issue of academic or intellectual freedom transcending the individual or the school system. For the officials had grown up in the secondary school world where teachers are employees; they said in effect that they had no trouble getting teachers and that it was unreasonable to expect them to investigate complaints about a man who hadn't actually entered the system. Had he actually started, I know they would have been protective of him as a member of the team, but they felt little responsibility to anything so abstract as freedom of opinion.

The case made me realize that, as the junior college movement spreads, we may see many twilight colleges, which appear free from the perspective of the high school but almost unprotected and even obscurantist from the perspective of the traditional private college. And at many of these junior colleges, as at some of the state or poorer private institutions, the chief academic freedom issues that arise do not involve ideas or associations, but rather the right of professors to flunk students who are plainly inadequate but who arguably may gain from postponing their entry on the job market.

What I have said should not be taken to mean that public institutions have no means of professional defense against the customer. Many of the big state institutions, if their presidents know their business, are more than a match for any single pressure group in the state; the University of Minnesota, for example, with its extensive services to the state, its great prestige, and its alumni holding virtually all state offices, is quite a power in its own right. (Lewis Dexter and Theodore Caplow have called other such cases to my attention.) But I am saying that the junior college which grows up from below, without an academic board of its own but bound to the secondary school system, may share the vulnerabilities of the latter and not create for the students who go there any sharp increase in illumination.

THE COUNTERVAILING POWER OF THE SCHOOLS

And yet, despite all I have said, despite all the pressures and pieties to which the schools must be subservient, we know from a great accumulation of public opinion data that differences of education differentiate Americans more sharply than any other single factor. The college-educated person, whatever his religion, race, or region, tends to become internationalist and cosmopolitan in outlook, to be liberal on civil liberties issues, and in general to be tolerant. (If he terms himself a conservative, it is rather because of his stand on economic and social welfare issues.) By contrast, the person who has gone only to grammar school is frequently xenophobic and suspicious—against giveaway programs and ties to foreign countries or to "foreigners" within this country. The high school and junior college graduates are between these extremes.

It is hard to separate out the effects of further schooling from the causes: we know from Kinsey's studies that the high school boy who will in all probability go to college already has different sexual patterns from the boy who will not. Income alone, apart from motivation, is not decisive, and it is clear that schooling attracts some and repels others at every point in the educational career. Certainly, one factor in the influence of high school and college is sheer size and movement; as the Junior Division *Bulletin* of the University of Nebraska states: college will bring "a mingling with young people from other communities and from foreign countries, whose backgrounds are different from yours and from whom you will learn just as they will learn from you"

(p. 7, 1955–56). We know that this growth of mutual understanding by no means happens as a regular thing, but, coupled with whatever broadening influence the teachers have, it does make the feeling of the bigot, that teachers and education in general must be watched, at least a comprehensible if not forgivable one. We who are college teachers are all too aware how little impact we and our ideas ordinarily have on the young, but the polls show us that we are part of an apparatus in our society that sorts people out into very different styles of life and thought.

And even at the secondary school level, as I have already implied, the teachers are not quite so powerless in controlling the customers as might appear. Any subordinate finds ways, along with his fellows, to frustrate superior authority, just as an Uncle Tom Negro can annoy his betters by being tardy, "stupid," and careless. In the "Blackboard Jungle" type schools studied by Howard C. Becker, the "old pro" teachers showed the young ones how to beat a child's head against the wall so it wouldn't show, and how, in general, to turn dreadful conditions into an apathetic sinecure. Likewise, Warren Peterson's study of Kansas City high school teachers gives many hints as to how, like other working groups, they set standards of performance, on the one hand, to make difficulties for the teacher who is insufficiently committed to her vocation and to her colleagues (he studied only the women) and, on the other hand, to put brakes on a "rate-buster" who becomes too devoted to her subject-matter or otherwise sets too exalted standards. Such solidarity often testifies to the very vulnerability of the group of colleagues, and it may be especially strong when there is little support for the teacher against parental pressure—little support from the principal or superintendent or school board. Understandably, this solidarity is seldom used to protect freedom or excellence of teaching, but in good trade union fashion to minimize exploitation, though it will be a long time before teachers, perhaps the most harassed of the big white-collar cadres, get a forty-hour week with a lessening of extra-curricular obligations and all the fringe benefits of the nurse, stenographer, dental technician, and airline hostess.[8]

Furthermore, public school teachers have done better than professors in organizing into unions which overleap the local community—this is, as just implied, in part because they are not academic, not attached to specific disciplines. In the state education departments, teachers have powerful lobbies. And in the National Education Association and the nationally known teachers colleges, the embattled teachers have begun to find support when they get into a local jam. The PTA often serves teachers as a public relations device, just as the school superintendent does. Indeed, the superintendent (and his wife) must be ceaselessly conciliatory, while fearing, like our foreign service officials, that he can never be diplomatic enough. Such men, as I have seen them, sometimes forget what they themselves think

[8] At the college level, lack of trustee or administrative protection can, under certain conditions, create in the faculty a notably resolute solidarity on academic freedom issues, and on such closely related issues as holding the football team to the same curricular demands as the rest. Indeed, I have the impression that a weak (but towards subordinates arbitrary) administration sometimes "inoculates" the faculty and readies it to cope with far more severe McCarthyite plagues, whereas a strong and just administration might be overprotective and leave the faculty defenseless if it should change or surrender. But such instances are more apt to occur at the procession's head, where faculty standards are high to begin with—and the professors therefore not too dependent on a particular job; at many colleges, a weak administration has the same effect, at best, that it would among the solidly united old-timers in a secondary school, and at worst exposes the faculty helplessly to local vigilantism.

or even who they are, lest they disturb some constituent, some paranoid parent, some self-styled "taxpayer."

THE INNER VULNERABILITY

The basic vulnerability of the teacher, however, is not, like the administrator, to the pressures from the parents and other veto groups in the community, damaging as these can be to his or her feeling of security and width of maneuver, but rather to the need to be liked by the children, the need to have evident and immediate response. The woman teacher particularly feels she is getting older while the children of course are not and although she may eventually resign herself to being a "character," feared and perhaps evaded, perhaps respected, she wants as long as possible to remain a "personality," warmly related to her charges. Unlike the research-minded professor, she cannot sublimate her pedagogical affects upon the general population; it is all very well for the university professor to tell her she should concentrate on her subject-matter and forget about "methods," but how is she to forget about the audience before whom, and only before whom, she performs?[9] Teachers have always cared whether they were

[9] College professors are, of course, not immune to student feelings about them. But great student popularity may make them suspect as unscholarly—and may cut into their time for research. (A school teacher with a captive classroom cannot share the sometimes wry pride of a professor who has only a few presumably select students.) However, at colleges where there is a great emphasis on undergraduate teaching—as a reaction to previous research-minded disregard—and especially where, as most directly at Antioch, the students have a say in hiring and retention of faculty, a professor may identify with a college as a residential community rather than with his discipline which is an impalpable community; in that case, he may be as vulnerable as any school teacher to the fluctuating fashions in student esteem. Some dialectic between the pressures from the immediate

liked by the children, but today, what with their developed social skills, they are more aware than hitherto whether or not they are liked, especially as the children, good operators that they are, include among *their* social skills the ability to exploit the adults' need for affection and approval—skills the young people have been taught in the child-centered middle-class home.[10]

In the movie "Rebel Without a Cause," there is a poignant scene in which the well-dressed California high school children are taken to a planetarium and lectured on the movements of the stars by an elderly man who obviously cares about stars. The kids are shown caring about each other—the stars are way over their heads; they couldn't care less, and the instructors, captives of their own captive audience, are prisoners of a ritual they cannot help but know is ridiculous.

---

audience and the unseen colleague group seems to me desirable, to protect both student and teacher from each other. Where, as in many graduate schools, there is little direct pressure from the students (particularly little against those professors who control either necessary skills or patronage), teaching can become extremely shoddy as the whole competitive pressure focuses on quantitative measures of research productivity and ignores ability to hand on old research traditions and inspire new ones. I think of this when I hear graduate professors denounce "methods courses" in normal schools and teachers colleges, for the denouncers could often themselves profit from courses in educational psychology, and are overprotected by their reputations and academic disciplines from the feedback of student trauma and justified complaint. Concerning graduate training, cf. my article, "Law and Sociology: Recruitment, Training, and Colleagueship," in *Stanford Law Review*, vol. 9 (1957), pp. 643–673.

[10] In at least the elementary grades in middle-class schools, the teacher can also (usually unconsciously) exploit the children's awareness of her needs for response; they will not, if enough leaders among the children are fond of her, want to disappoint her. See Jules Henry's discussion in "Docility, or Giving Teacher What She Wants," *Journal of Social Issues*, vol. 11 (1955), pp. 33–41; I am indebted to Professor Henry for his as yet unpublished classroom observations.

No wonder that under such conditions teachers have sought to compete by coming to terms with topics hopefully closer to student concerns. This is one of the reasons history is often dropped in favor of the social studies amalgam. Indeed, though life has not always treated them too well, school teachers have often interpreted the progressive education movement as a mandate to meet life head on (rather than retreat from it as many college professors are able to do), a mandate to bring it into the classroom and cope with it as best they can.

THE DIALECTIC OF PROGRESSIVISM

The pioneers of progressive education were, in many cases, courageous people, reformers willing to do battle against the entrenched prejudices and apathies of parents and school administrations and teachers. Heirs of the Enlightenment, they could believe that, whatever setbacks occurred, the cause of progress would win; and many could also believe that only the stuffy bourgeois stood in their way and that the working class, were it to become educated and informed, would be on their side. Some of them did not live to face the conflicts which have occurred with the immense increase in the proportion who attend high school. Progressive education has, however, turned out to mean quite different things at Putney or Shady Hill Country Day or the Little Red School House and at many city and suburban high schools in middle-class areas throughout the country— schools into which, despite all the wild and absurd attacks on John Dewey, the progressive movement has continued to spread. It has spread in part because there are funds enough and school systems large and entrenched enough for some moderate experimentation.

But it has also spread because, as already indicated, it offers the schools a way of appearing up to date and closer to the students' alleged interests, while abandoning subjects like languages and ancient or European history which reached fewer students but made (when even passably taught) greater demands on those they reached. In other words, progressive education now serves in many prosperous communities to deprive the more studious of challenges they could well endure and profit from, and to give their teachers a high-minded excuse for being distracted from devotion to their subjects, in exchange for devotion to cultivating an harmonious and democratic classroom atmosphere.[11] While progressivism at its best is still liberating, because it is individuating and compels specific attention to the specific child in the totality of its setting, in a large urban or suburban system a small dose of it is often a way to preclude a larger dose.

It has today become necessary to stress that the progressive reformers did not desire any such result as this. They did not want to dilute the intellectuality of the existing schools, but to encourage a less narrow and doctrinaire intellectuality, and to add to it. For example, if one reads Lucy Sprague Mitchell's eloquent book, *Two Lives*, about her husband, the economist Wesley Mitchell, and herself, one can readily see the abundant human qualities she aimed at in her pioneering work in elementary education: she wanted, not emotional and

[11] One reason for this is that progressive education began—notably, in Maria Montessori's work—at the kindergarten and elementary school level, and spread from there into the higher grades. As Lyman Bryson has argued in correspondence, it can be a snare at the higher levels because "it too generously substituted motor thinking, which the child usually loves, for abstract thinking which he has to learn to do"—though he agrees that, given the great differences in native endowment, not all teenage young people can or should be made to learn to do so (and, contrariwise, some children do spontaneously enjoy abstract thinking).

group-anchored life at the expense of intellect, but as the support of it. All this tends to be overlooked even by the historian Arthur Bestor, in his only moderately savage traditionalist criticisms of the public schools, and willfully overlooked by many others who look down their noses at Teachers College at Columbia and at all those they sneer at as "educationists." For these critics, the dilemmas of democratic education simply can be willed away if only one could restore the classical curriculum, and discover an elite to administer and another to endure it.

The "Unreality" of the British Public School

Let us now, however, in order to gain some perspective on these contemporary arguments, step back into the past and observe the British public (i.e., private) schools of an earlier day—schools as buffered from popular pressure as one can imagine any school to be outside of a totalitarian state.[12] As soon as we do look, we run into an apparent paradox, namely, that places like Eton, with their games of cricket and their classical curricula, were traditionally very remote from life—yet their graduates seemed to be prepared to cope with the British Empire. How can we explain this? There may, of course, not be any connection, or indeed the schools may have been dysfunctional and what was achieved by their graduates may have been despite their education. Yet an alternative possibility remains, namely that it was the very unrealistic and in that sense unprogressive education these schools gave that was a factor in

[12] There is plenty of evidence that the British now face conflicts analogous to ours. Cf., e.g., H. T. Himmelweit, A. H. Halsey, and A. N. Oppenheim, "The Views of Adolescents on Some Aspects of the Social Class Structure," *British Journal of Sociology*, vol. 3 (1952), pp. 148–172; also James Bryant Conant, *Education and Liberty* (Cambridge, Mass.: Harvard University Press, 1953), chapter 1 and sources there cited.

their success—if we grant for the moment that to get and run an Empire while civilizing the British Isles is a form of success. Taken early from home and thrust into an all-male world, the students were also intellectually thrust into Greece and Rome. By this emphasis on the classics (especially after Thomas Arnold's reforms), the parochial Englishman became, if drily and vicariously, cultivated and sure. Tremendous demands for work were put upon him. He was taught an upper-class accent and posture which were portable symbols of status, not tied to the land in the old feudal fashion and not dependent upon money, but dependent rather on having enough money or drive back of one to have attended such a school and enough hardihood to have graduated. It has been much easier in Britain to become a lord—which only takes money and good Party works—than to acquire, after school days are over, the more intangible symbol of R.P., "received pronunciation"—the symbol by which, wherever around the globe they might meet, the British ex-schoolboys could recognize each other.

These schools marked, and often marred, a man for life, in the very way he talked and carried himself, and for him the classical allusion might serve as a passport to any position in much the way that the Chinese mandarin's knowledge of Confucius could serve him; in fact, I am inclined to think that one could have exchanged Chinese and British education without altering their impact in either country. Both curricula were sharply marked out from the life about one, and thus enabled one to transcend that life. The Englishman in India could go out in the noonday sun, like the mad dog in the song, because in school he had been detached, as it were, from his own body, his own climate—a very impressive thing for the Indians, if not always a very happy thing for the Englishman. The code of fair play, I might add, was equally a matter of impersonality and self-detachment, and equally impressive; it has, as we know, left its mark on such great Indian leaders as Nehru. But I cannot emphasize too strongly that this school system was not designed *as* a system; it was not, though the masters knew they were drilling an elite, aimed, for the most part, at these practical results, which came (assuming that in fact they did come—an unproven hypothesis) as an almost arbitrary by-product.

Class Snobbery as a Defense for Educational Values

The protection of these schools from public and democratic pressure was also not on the whole the result of conscious contrivance, but rather of the arrogance, snobbery, and social distance built into British life—and these are high prices to pay for liberty. The snobbery is typified by the Victorian home, with its high ceilings downstairs and its great distances, while the servants stifled on the top floor; such a home was not built for easy approachability and communication. British mothers were more limited by their sex and code from complaining to a headmaster than American mothers are from complaining to an Army colonel in whose regiment their son is serving. It is testimony to the greater openness and equality of American life that parents are willing to beard a school principal or even a university president as no one in a Continental country would dare to do.

By the same token, the American colonel, principal, and president see themselves, like any company president, as the chief public relations officers of their outfits, engaged in winning friends and placating enemies. John Paul Moulton, a student in the Department of Education at the University of Chicago, recently asked a group of secondary school teachers a series of questions bearing on their image of the relation between the

school and the community. One of the questions asked
was what they would do if they were president of a college and a parent came to complain about a textbook as
scandalous. Most of the teachers saw the problem as one
in good public relations, assumed the parent had a right
to complain, and suggested ways of investigating the
matter, such as appointing a committee. Not one suggested what would undoubtedly be a British reaction:
"Take your child out if you like, but don't bother me!"
The British public schools could go counter to majority
patterns in Britain in much the same way that, until
recently, the upper-class Englishman could be as eccentric as he liked, including becoming a Communist, because of his secure lodgement at the top.

THE LIMITS OF COUNTER-CYCLICAL ACTION

In this country, the class structure is much less clear-
cut, and the schools, even the private schools, have much
less opportunity to be protected in an enclave of social
arrogance against majority pressures and majority defini-
tions of what "real life" is like. Nor can schools defend
themselves in idiosyncracy simply on the basis of having
always been like that—we cannot reach back to the
thirteenth century (save all too gruesomely in some of
our fake Gothic architecture!) and defend the classical
curriculum as part of the order of things. Thus, our
schools have fewer defenses against being realistic and
close to life—and this is true even of our Catholic and
Lutheran parochial schools, which in so many ways must
fashion themselves on the public schools if they are to
stay in business.

As a result, the opportunity of the schools for counter-
cyclical influence is quite limited. Even so, just as
Keynesian economics would have the banks and the gov-

ernment save in a time of inflation and spend in a time
of depression, so the schools, in selecting among the demands on them from their various publics, have some
very modest opportunities to oppose "life" in its momentary excesses. In the British context, for example,
or its offshoots and rare analogues in this country, it
would make sense to be preoccupied with social skills,
and to encourage more scope for the emotional and
aesthetic aspects of life, for in Britain in general these
aspects have been at a discount. In fact, there is an impressive array of British novelists and poets who suffered
torment in public school, as their autobiographies make
clear. The progressive reformers, both in England and
in the United States, attacked the emotional blindness
and cruelty of such old-fashioned schools, and their job
is by no means done in either country. There are still
schools where the arts are thought to be for sissies (despite the enormous impact of Surette and other crusad-
ers for school music), just as there are still colleges in
the Ivy League where the arts are thought to be mainly
for the museum.

THE ALTERED CONTEXT OF PROGRESSIVE EDUCATION

Yet I need hardly recount the extent to which the
out-of-school context has changed for millions (though
still probably a small minority) of children in the last
decades. There is a boom in pianos, a boom in LP records, a boom in finger paints. Young people at home
are listened to—they are no longer seen and not heard;
at least in the larger cities and the educated middle
classes, the home is a communications laboratory. No
longer needing to do chores around the house, children
hold such jobs as soda jerker, baby sitter, camp coun-
selor, in many of which they learn poise and how to get

along with others. They can and do use the movies, comics, TV, magazines such as *Seventeen* and *Glamour*, as well as each other's example, to learn proper social behavior—proper, that is, for their set, whatever their parents may think. No one, I might add, should sneer at these social proficiencies: if one compares American young people today with their counterparts a generation ago, or with young Europeans today, one is struck by their maturity, by their understanding of themselves, each other, and adults. Yet some of our schools, correcting for deficiencies of an earlier day, are giving many of these youngsters what amounts to post-graduate education in social relations when what they most need is something very different, namely, protection for certain long-term intellectual and humanistic interests that are momentarily under pressure and apt to be squeezed out.

Some teachers, to be sure, fight a strong rear-guard action in defense of high intellectual and artistic standards, but others find in the progressive education movement rationalizations for lowering standards and for coming to terms with the general level of inclination in the classroom.[13] In this impact of progressivism, we can

---

[13] I am aware that there is danger of chronic nostalgia in such observations. As I have said earlier, students were rowdy and unintellectual in previous generations when but a fraction went beyond grammar school; many teachers were blind to the variety of student dispositions and even untrained in the classical curriculum they were supposed to teach. Nepotism, which sponsored into the school system many cultivated spinster relatives of local big-wigs, also (as my colleague, Peter Blau, has emphasized) found places for incompetents and discouraged meritorious people with better training. Control of certification into the public schools by state education departments was a response to real abuses as well as a characteristic move towards professionalization with all its ambivalent blessings.

One could find many examples of laxity in the nineteenth century in the histories of education or of particular colleges; one that sounds very up to date in some ways comes from Emerson's journal (July 24, 1863):

see something of a short circuit in the communication of ideas, rather like some of those we touched upon in my first lecture in connection with the diffusion of high culture, and in my second in connection with general education. For as I have already said, progressive education in its original impetus was counter-cyclical: it was an all-out attack on the Colonel Blimps of the school world, on cruelty and one-sidedness, on uniformity of curriculum and pacing. This attack, though first developed in a few private schools here and abroad, was resisted by the older type of academic prep school, such as St. George's, St. Timothy's, and Rosemary Hall—not to speak of the military schools and the convent schools, some of which aped the worst features of the British public school. Conservative and conventional parents of high status also resisted progressivism, as did many teachers. In this setting, the movement put pressure on all concerned, on opponents as well as proponents; it led to animated, if at times confusing, discussion of the educational process, and it was frequently productive both for teachers and parents who sought to keep up with the new ideas and for the children of the move-

---

"I went to Dartmouth College, and found the same old Granny system which I met there twenty-five years ago. The President has an aversion to emulation, as injurious to the character of the pupils. He therefore forbids the election of members into the two literary societies by merit, but arranges that the first scholar alphabetically on the list shall be assigned to the Adelphi, and the second to the Mathesians, and the third to the Adelphi, and the fourth to the Mathesians; and so on. Every student belonging to the one or the other. 'Well, but there is a first scholar in the class, is there not, and he has the first oration at Commencement?' 'Oh, no, the parts are assigned by lot.' The amiable student who explained it added that it tended to remove disagreeable excitement from the societies. I answered, 'Certainly, and it would remove more if there were no college at all.' I recommended morphine in liberal doses at the College Commons." *The Heart of Emerson's Journals*, Bliss Perry, ed. (Cambridge, Mass.: Harvard University Press, 1926), p. 299. I am indebted to Fred Somkin, Esq., for this reference.

ment who strove to understand and sympathize even with their "backward" parents.

Today, many parents who themselves attended conventional private schools prefer, even when they can easily afford otherwise, to send their children to public schools which they regard as more progressive; they want, moreover, to give their children an exposure to a wider range of social-class encounters (an experiment, I might add, often doomed to defeat because the greater heterogeneity of the public school leads, if not to segregation by suburb, then to severe class stratification within the school—for these reasons, Groton and Brearly are presently at least as democratic within the walls as most public schools I know).

Most private schools, however, have not been wholly immune to these wider social tendencies. For instance, they are encouraging a greater equality, both between students and staff and among the students; they are broadening the base of activities in the school to include not only sports and science and the classics but also the arts, social studies, and counseling, and they are making an effort to play down scholastic competitiveness. These developments do the private schools credit, yet there is a certain loss to the educational scene as a whole by their refusal to turn old vices, such as snobbery and overintellectualism, into new virtues at a time when all other schools that can financially afford it are moving in a similar direction. For the result is isomorphism—the same loss of variety we earlier discussed on the level of the colleges. If schools are not to be experimental by design, then we can at least hope that they will remain experimental and different by default (as Rip Van Winkle, a bore in his own day, might, in his delayed awakening, be today a new and interesting kind of man).

Equality and Age

There are two traditional differences I want to discuss, one briefly and the other at greater length. The
first is the problem of the age difference between teachers and students to which I have already adverted. In
an earlier day, along with social class snobbery there was
gerontocracy, and teachers considered the students as
miniature adults who had to come to terms with the
adult world as the teachers defined it—or else. In such
a system, differences were stressed rather than similarities, and teachers emphasized their intellectual superiority and protected themselves behind the crust of age.
How harmful this often was, I need hardly stress; children were sometimes cruelly exploited, forced into a
dead passivity or a blind rebellion. Today, by contrast,
it often seems that the teachers, and adults more generally, wish they could eradicate this remaining "undemocratic" distinction of age which the flow of the
generations remorselessly reproduces; they feel it unfair
to take advantage, as they would feel they were doing,
of the greater knowledge that occasionally accompanies
greater age; they prefer to come to terms with the young
in the expressive domain—the domain, that is, where it
would appear that we can all be human together—
rather than making demands in the cognitive one.

The result in many ways has been good for both par-
ties to the generational dialectic. The teachers have
stayed "younger"; the children have become affectively
mature more quickly and with somewhat less strain—
in fact, educators and others have discovered hitherto
unrealized potentials for expressiveness in the children.
But there is a loss, too, in this development. As other
differences of condition diminish, it seems to me proper
counter-cyclical policy to emphasize again the positive
aspects of age-grading. I would like to see teachers be-

come more adult in the model of excellence they present to children, and hence in the expectations they have of them intellectually, leaving the pal function to other agencies in the society, or to themselves on another occasion. Correspondingly, I am inclined to think —a point I shall return to later—that teen-agers could well afford to become slightly less adult in such practices as going steady and holding jobs which are intellectually and artistically meaningless.

COEDUCATION AND THE IMITATION OF LIFE

The other traditional difference which is under pressure exists in the non-coeducational schools and colleges, and in discussing it I hope I can clarify further what I mean by counter-cyclical thinking. Since for obvious reasons boys at schools like Exeter or colleges like Princeton are less worried about sex-segregation than are girls at equivalent institutions, I would prefer to draw my examples from the girls' colleges. I have had the opportunity of visiting a number of these recently, from Smith and Mt. Holyoke and the Women's College of the University of North Carolina in the East, to Mills in the West, and wherever I have gone the students have been quite generally full of misgivings about a non-coeducational school; it was, they said, "unnatural," "a nunnery," a "poor preparation for life and marriage," and so on. At these colleges, this outlook was about the only topic on which there was uniformity, for the groups to whom I talked struck me as exceptionally diverse in appearance and opinion and talent—far more so than the girls at comparable coed schools. At the latter, the girls, though no less well educated, have always seemed to me more subdued, indeed more uniform; this is the case, I fear, even at the College of the University of

Chicago where girls on the whole conceal their talents less than at many places. This is understandable, because the girls in the classroom worry not only about what the boys would say about what they said, but also about what the other girls would think about what the boys would think—a feedback to daunt all but the most courageous or insensitive![14] While from the perspective of Smith or Vassar, the coed schools cultivate easygoing camaraderie with boys as against the artificiality of week-end visits and proms, what the camaraderie seems to me often to accomplish is to anticipate by four years the girl's marriage to a boy whom she will assist in his career by sacrificing hers. The best women's colleges appear to give their students an opportunity to "be themselves" five days a week—and then to vary that diet (by being somebody else!) on weekends and holidays.

To be sure, no reader of Theodore Newcomb's study of Bennington, *Personality and Social Change*, can remain immune to the problem posed for girls who ac-

---

[14] There is more to it, of course, than such relatively late feedback. An example comes from the following story told by a fourth-grade girl to Ann Jernberg, a graduate student at Chicago:

"She was in the house sitting in a chair and she decided she had nothing to do. So she got very bored and she went up to her room and she looked around for toys she might play with, but she didn't find anything she felt like doing, so she went outside.

"Then she went over to her friend's house . . . asked her friend to come out. So they decided they would play jump rope. So they jumped rope for a while and then her friend had to go in and eat and so did she . . . and so they went in, ate, and then she . . . they went to bed after that. And then she told her mother they really had a lot of fun that day. But that's not really right. That wasn't really a very exciting story. If I had told you one about a boy it would have been a much more exciting story . . . Like: A little boy climbed a tree and got stuck up there and a woodcutter came to chop down the tree, and he tried to tell the woodcutter but he couldn't hear. It would end alright but it would be more exciting. Boys do more things that are exciting, like climb trees and fish. Girls do that too I guess, but not as exciting. Like boys would catch big fish or fall in a pond or something."

tually develop, as many girls at such a college do, beyond their home-town boy-friends and home-town parents—or even beyond Williams or Dartmouth boy-friends. I recall especially one girl Newcomb describes who had absorbed Bennington's then rather advanced ideas on race relations and politics and who, when she went home for Christmas, tried to introduce these ideas when she was out on a date with her steady. The latter said: "Have another drink; you'll get over it." One could argue that the girl would have been better off if she'd been taught merely to drink and not to think, but if girls had been brought up in recent generations only to the intellectual level the marriage market was thought to be able to carry, men today as well as the girls would suffer from it—not to speak of the whole quality of our intellectual life.

Because of the changes in life outside the schools and colleges, however, the advantages of coeducation have almost become superfluous in recent years. A few decades ago, in the non-coed schools, boy-girl relations were often over-formal and excessively glamour-oriented; neither boys nor girls had institutional support in learning the give-and-take of everyday life; segregation might produce nuns and monks (who might then react to claustrophobia by a violent binge). The career girl at that time often did not marry and, as Katherine Hepburn's roles have reminded us in countless movies, regretted it too late. Today, however, our grammar schools and our high schools encourage more mixing of the sexes than even our colleges once did. Indeed all people in the United States—even Bennington or Smith girls—go steady younger and marry earlier and more often than they used to, and the problem is no longer one of promoting more "naturalness" between the sexes but rather of retaining enough constraint and formality in our social life—and perhaps a little time for the cul-

tivation of individuality and difference in both the
sexes. Under these circumstances it would be a real
loss if the non-coed type of school should disappear
entirely.[15]

Please remember that I am not talking about everybody. Not all girls or boys need a moratorium from each
other, or a good alibi for not being gregarious or date-
crazy; others, indeed, may need a moratorium from the
curriculum which may too easily convince them they are
untalented—convince them of their total worthlessness
when the verdict on them is actually a very limited and
parochial one.

SOURCES OF VARIETY IN THE SCHOOLS

To many people such an outcome will seem most unlikely, for they are only familiar with the more typical
pattern in which intellectual achievement has negative
consequences for prestige—or at least ambivalent ones
—and in which the values of the teachers count for little
in the total rank order of the school. In this pattern,
young people suffer less because the curriculum op-
presses them than because they oppress each other. Yet
a truly counter-cyclical theory of education would have

[15] In this connection, it is striking that, in some circles, the
favorite colleges for girls are coming to be Oberlin, Swarthmore,
Reed, Antioch. All are coed; all are relatively small; all have
about them a certain plainness, even asceticism; all but Reed are
outside metropolitan areas. Those who choose these colleges are
doing so in many cases in preference both to the traditional daisy-
chain schools and the better-known state universities; they sometimes choose them in the face of parental or school-guidance
pressures. In doing so, they represent what in some ways are the
finest qualities of today's young Americans: simplicity, cooperative-
ness, tolerance, modesty, seriousness (these colleges notably turn
out good scientists and artists). Yet even this model of excellence
needs to be confronted with alternative models such as the best
non-coeducational colleges represent.

to try to take account of both possibilities. Indeed, it would have to see that students can be damaged almost as much by success in school as by failure, for the one who is a success may be overpersuaded of his abilities along certain limited lines and underacquainted with many aspects of himself and of his setting.

Single versus Multiple Criteria

One possibility of diminishing these risks is to do whatever can be done to encourage a variety of paths to a variety of types of success, rather than offering a monolithic definition of it. And perhaps the ideal school would be one where the cyclical and counter-cyclical both existed within it. In fact, my colleague James Coleman argues almost the same thing: that high schools do least damage when there are many competing criteria for success—for example, the brains, the athletes, the jazz-fans, the girl-fans, the literary set, and so on, not excluding the chess club and the hot-rodders. In such a setting, a boy who has, let us say, both athletic and musical gifts will not be forced to stress the former alone and neglect the latter, because in his school only athletic success is considered worth while. Indeed, where there are many competing avenues to recognition, no single one is apt to destroy the possibilities for differentiation by subjecting everyone to a unidimensional definition of what matters in life. To be sure, such considerations assume that young people will not go against the fast-moving stream of the high school culture; and of course some will: a rare few because they are already genuinely autonomous, and others because they cannot play the given games at all.

Likewise, Coleman and I assume that not many parents can or will support their children in strongly held values which go counter to those of the high school; all the things Margaret Mead has said, in *The School in American Culture* and in other writings, concerning the way children are usually one-up on their parents, having had more, or more modern schooling, are to the point here. Moreover, the most monolithic high school, as the Lynds pointed out in their *Middletown* volumes, refract adult patterns of competition and conformity; and most parents, however they may deplore the elements of "excess" and caricature in the high school, will either judge their children by the same standards for popularity and prestige the high school employs, or, even though sympathetic to their children as they struggle and suffer, will not be able to provide any alternative standards.

The Social Security of Going Steady

The custom of going steady which has become the major dating pattern in so many high schools may in some measure be related to the severity of the high school's definition of success; for going steady is, among many other benefits, social insurance against failure; it appears as a stabilizing factor in a setting where the individual feels he has no control over the definition of the values he must live by. In contrast to this, a high school setting which frees young people from such dependence and allows small groups to define their own excellences may not put such pressure on the students to anchor themselves. Obviously, just as the high schools refract wider patterns of adult culture, while at the same time reshaping these, so such a shift as that towards going steady and teen-age marriage is not to be explained by any single element in the high school; certainly it reflects more universal combinations of relative social maturity and social insecurity combined with full employment and freer sexuality. Yet here, too, some high schools—those with but a single glaring spotlight—constrain their students more to a uniform dating fashion than do others.[16]

Safety in Numbers?

A very small school is unlikely, under most conditions, to provide adequate variety, for better or worse; Coleman points out that school consolidation not only allows the potential science fans to come together by sorting out and developing those aspects of themselves that strike a chord in others, but also the potential delinquents who, in a rural school, might not have developed their gifts for sabotage. Moreover, some children may feel that the huge place that offers everything may lack something—just as a supermarket has not the charm nor quality of the butcher shop, the French pastry shop, and the Italian grocer. That is, if all schools were supermarkets, they would tend towards uniformity vis-à-vis each other, despite greater differentiation within.[17]

[16] I recognize, of course, that couples who go steady can and do shift their partners over time, though this may involve the complex diplomacy of a double divorce. I recognize, too, the argument that going steady leads to real knowledge of the other, as against the mink-coated knowledge of those who play the field. Even so, I feel there is more constraint than freedom in the pattern, though I am troubled by the constrictions imposed by the demand that one go steady or be out in the cold; I do not share the alarmist view of many of my generation, biased by nostalgia for a different experience and blind to emergent forms and values. For a study of contemporary college dating preferences which indicates the vogue of the natural and sincere, as against the rating-dating values described a generation ago by Willard Waller, see Robert Blood, Jr., "Uniformities and Diversities in Campus Dating Preferences," *Marriage and Family Living*, vol. 18 (1956), pp. 37–45.

[17] Applying such considerations to our College at Chicago, for example, leads me to argue that we would be mistaken to pursue a course of trying to "normalize" the College, to make it more like the typical university college as some would like to see us do. I argue this way when I think of the national scene,

Captive and Free Audiences

We would simplify our task if we could increase the mobility of young people in seeking out a high school —and a college—whose particular excellences and weaknesses bear some relation to their own personal qualities. Even at the high school level, more can be done to broaden, with modern transport, the orbits in which young people make choices, as well as the intelligence with which such choices are made. In New York City a child of high school age can try to get into the specialized schools of top quality such as the High School of Music and Art, the several schools of science, or Hunter High School, the top-flight liberal arts school for girls. In many school systems, however, it is only what one might term "downward idiosyncracy" that entitles a child living at home to attend a special class or school, such as one for retarded or deaf children.

And of course the child is still a captive audience for the family, and ordinarily for the neighborhood school. If we wait until he can move about, he may not want to move in anything but a geographic sense. As an aspect of the Harvard Social Mobility Project, Joseph A. Kahl interviewed the parents of a group of Boston high school seniors who were bright enough to go to college, who could afford it, but who did not plan to go. These interviews showed how strongly many parents felt against the idea of college, with such arguments as: You can get a good job without going to college, and you forget, don't you, even what you learn in high school!

Of course, children of such egregiously practical parents have gone on to college in spite of them, thanks

---

and the way in which Chicago has served as a beacon for many schools. And yet I realize that in the Hutchins regime bright students could on occasion be harmed by having too many easy plaudits for their brightness—just as at other schools they might have been harmed by having their sharpness held against them.

often in recent years to the Army. Sometimes it will turn out that they have had the good luck to meet a teacher who served as a model of excellence, a model transcending anything available in the home. The teacher's mobility made up for the pupil's lack of it, and eventually led to the pupil's mobility as well. Everett Hughes, however, as the result of a number of studies of the school-teaching profession, is inclined to think that teachers today, while better trained on the whole, are less apt to hold really high aims themselves or to inspire them in their students. They themselves have not been inspired, for in their teacher training institutions there seldom appears much countervailing power against modest aims—seldom an encounter with teachers who have genuine enthusiasm for learning and discovery. Moreover, as happens in every profession, many of those who do emerge from a teachers college with glowing idealism encounter in their first teaching jobs the most depressing schools, whose principals cannot recruit experienced teachers; some never recover from the shock. Naturally enough, such teachers want to escape the slums and teach "nice" children in "nice" neighborhoods, but even beyond this drive, the Hughes-sponsored studies indicate a general preference for the middling school, not too experimental and not noted for its bright or gifted children—the school where the parents have had a high school education only, so that they may look up to the teacher and not question her authority (Professor Wilbur Brookover has studied school districts where even lower-class schools are preferred, because the parents offer so little interference). Given the community pressures on teachers which we have briefly sketched in this lecture, such a search for a relatively unchallenging school setting is to be expected. However, to the extent that teachers and parents present a relatively united front of mediocrity, the children will be without recourse, and the cycle will repeat itself.

REVERSING THE CYCLE

Nevertheless, the hope for countervailing power against mediocrity in the schools can count on certain tendencies in our society to provide a cadre of devoted principals and teachers who will want to work precisely in the off-beat schools, and who will seek challenge rather than routine. There are a number of young people who no longer seek fame and monetary success or even ease of life but look for a life of service in the more challenging jobs that service people or ideas rather than things. Rejecting uncongenial intellectuality, they want to work with people, to help people; they are less concerned than most college professors are with sheer mental endowment and more concerned with personality and with the total gamut of the child's development. Some will become psychiatrists, but others, democratic in spirit, uncompetitive, unethnocentric, will become teachers and may find as great a challenge in working, for example, with slum children as missionaries in an earlier day found in working with preliterate tribes. Indeed, as the ministry loses its attraction for the zealous, or gets redefined as another sort of working with people, the schools for the ethnically and intellectually underprivileged—indeed, the schools in general —find themselves with new possibilities for recruitment. Thus, while understandably a very large proportion of teachers will continue to look to their profession for status, it seems to me that we can expect an increase in the ranks of those teachers who enter the profession not in search of status but in search of a meaningfully useful life.[18] There are now many such teachers in the private schools, and a great many more in the public schools than uninterested parents and overbearing school boards "deserve."

AMBIGUITIES OF COUNTER-CYCLICAL THINKING

It is less, however, the problem of finding devoted teachers who care for excellence, than one of defining what is excellent, that appears to me to complicate major improvement in the diversification of school patterns. In the financial field, counter-cyclical thinking can aim at tasks which, if not simple, are at least unidimensional: we know, more or less, what depression and prosperity are. And while a Schumpeter might favor the creative destruction of a depression (along with businessmen worried about wage rigidity and inflation), Keynesian thinking has made such headway that Republicans and Democrats alike are committed to stabilization and full employment policies: to advocate deflation other than in allopathic or placebo doses is political suicide. But in the field of education there is no such commitment to ironing out the swings in the trend cycle. The Great Depression was for some of its victims

[18] Let me make clear that I am not pleading for life-long self-sacrifice here. While I think it is a good thing to conscript the young for a cause for a short time, I have serious doubts even about a voluntary life sentence. When I spent a summer with the Grenfell Mission in Labrador many years ago, I observed that those who sacrificed themselves for a longer period than two years frequently ended up with no self left—and, save for a rare saint or two, they were apt to take out their frustrations on the natives. Just as I would not expect a banker who believed a depression was coming, and who had read John Maynard Keynes, to invest his personal fortune as a way of increasing purchasing power, so I do not expect individual teachers or school officials to pay the entire cost of a counter-cyclical movement.

scarcely worse than the rigid feeding schedule for infants prescribed by pediatricians in the post-Watson era was for many children subjected to it; the Great Boom of the fifties was scarcely worse for the adults it disoriented than the rigid permissiveness prescribed by a later generation of parent-proctors was for children brought up by its tenets; yet the result of these excesses has not been to produce an educational program of resistance to such changes.[19]

Some years ago, a thoughtful professor of education wrote me: "If society *is* becoming more and more other-directed, why should not the school, its agency, do likewise?" She was not wholly convinced that it should; though educators do often talk about "adjustment to life," they are still apt to be selective about what they regard as life. It is easier, as I have already implied, to tinker with a rediscount rate or other financial lever of Keynesian stabilization policy than with the fates of children whom one wants to have go counter to life in some of its more flaccid or diluted aspects. But I am convinced that young people miss something if they are not called on for any sacrifice or challenge.

The present disposition in school and college is to turn out whole men, all-round men, free of the often grievous one-sidedness of the *Wunderkind* of another day.[20] The young people themselves, of course, accept

[19] Working with the Infant Care Bulletins issued by the Department of Labor, Martha Wolfenstein has described in detail some of the implications of the many shifts from 1914 to the present. See "Fun Morality: An Analysis of Recent American Child-Training Literature," pp. 168–178 in *Childhood in Contemporary Cultures*, ed. by Margaret Mead and Martha Wolfenstein (Chicago: Univ. of Chicago Press, 1955), chapter 10.

[20] I don't mean to imply here, contrary to the evidence gathered by Lewis Terman, Robert J. Havighurst, and others concerning gifted children, that the exceptional child is necessarily one-sided: usually he has more of everything. Nevertheless, his gifts for

the same ideal. It is implicit in their nearly universal desire for marriage and children and a well-rounded family life; it is implicit also, during their school and college days, in their insistence on holding paying jobs even when they don't need them financially—jobs in most cases unrelated to career ambitions but useful in acquainting them early with responsibility (useful also, for the privileged, as cross-class experience); it is implicit in the relative lack of resentment against military service.[21]

These young people are unwilling to sacrifice the fullness of life for one aspect of life, and this represents in many ways a sounder set of values than that of earlier generations who would often sacrifice overmuch for money, respectability, or distinction. Even so, what we sometimes find is that the "whole man," who has not had any encouragement at home or in school to push certain great talents and neglect others, is not necessarily the happy man: his life may lack drama and contrast, and his wholeness may atrophy out of its very evenness and comfort.[22] Counter-cyclical policy would see to it

leadership, citizenship, and easy affability can be developed at the expense of attention to his artistic or intellectual potential, since the energies of even the gifted do have limits.

[21] I am indebted for some not wholly reliable information on the goals of young people to interviews done by *Time* with 183 members of the Class of 1955 at twenty colleges throughout the country; the interviews have been analyzed in terms of the students' ambitions for the future by Robin Jackson, Research Associate of the Center for the Study of Leisure. See my article, "The Found Generation," *American Scholar*, vol. 26 (1956), pp. 421–431; and, to similar effect, Russell Lynes, "What Has Succeeded Success?" *Mademoiselle*, Sept. 1954, p. 101.

[22] We can compare the devout belief in integration and wholeness in individuals with the movement for interdisciplinary integration discussed in the previous lecture. It was there suggested that, in construction of theories, scholars were afraid of leaving out any relevant facet; thus, they avoided commitment to the most significant (and previously neglected) aspects of reality: each intellectual veto group was entitled to representation on joint projects and in the very structure of knowledge. Much

that even the virtue of wholeness did not sweep all before it, and that there would be some institutions where those who dared to be one-sided would find their gifts encouraged, their values affirmed.

These are some of the moral ambiguities and practical uncertainties of a counter-cyclical policy for our schools. Such a policy is subject to many of the criticisms that have been brought against Kenneth Galbraith's comparable concept of countervailing power—a concept in which the veto groups of political and economic life serve, with a modicum of government assistance, to balance each other, to cancel out each other's potential for harmful domination. Even within this narrow range, educational leverage, as I have indicated, is less easily discovered than economic; for one thing, in contrast to the relative centralization of business and investment decisions, responsibility for education is greatly decentralized among thousands of school boards, PTAs, teacher associations, textbook lobbies, state education departments, teachers colleges of all levels of excellence, and so on (the Supreme Court is finding how tenuous is control of education either by the Federal Courts or by national opinion when local communities resist). I see no ready way to institutionalize counter-cyclical thinking in education, even though when a lukewarm caricature of progressivism has spread to many of the less well-to-do public schools, we may also expect that new developments which cope with its inadequacies will also be publicized: as any teacher can testify, there is no want of journals (or Fund for the Advancement of Education

---

in the same way, every capacity of the student is, so to speak, "represented" within him by a pressure group from the outside, telling him not to overlook his civic, religious, athletic, or cooperative skills. It would be "unfair" of him to listen to the voice of only one of his gifts. This "democracy of talents" within the gifted often leads them to spread themselves too thinly in attempting to placate every internalized veto group.

programs) to bring the news of what is happening elsewhere to those who cannot get to summer school.

Counter-cyclical strategy, moreover, is only one aspect of an educational philosophy. Taken alone, it could become (as my colleague Jack Getzels points out) merely the "negation of negation," inherently relativistic and opposing new developments which appear "excessive" although a longer perspective would show them to be fruitful.[23] For counter-cyclical action can accomplish no more than to moderate swings of educational fashion in the avant-garde while bringing the rear guard and the home guard a bit nearer to the former. It is forced to take for granted the vested interests—the very vested existence—of the schools, and the prevailing patterns of career choice out of which teachers and scholars arise, while hoping to enlighten in small degree those interests and choices. Like balance-of-power thinking in international and domestic struggles, it may at times be the best we can do, especially in times when fanaticism is a greater danger than stalemate. Yet to a person who imaginatively becomes aware of the enormous waste of talent in our (or any) country, of the triviality of most academic and school busywork, of the erosion of creativity among both teachers and taught, counter-cyclical action must seem like the merest tinkering.

Thus, perhaps paradoxically, counter-cyclical policy depends for its efficacy on the presence of people in the schools who think otherwise—radical reconstructionists who have a program of their own, not premised on applying or resisting the givens already available. It is not even enough to see to it—great as the advance would be—that schools which now see their function as that of imitating life and preparing for it, take as the life they have in mind no mean slice, but a wide-angled cosmo-

[23] For further discussion of these dangers, cf. my article, "Values in Context," in *Individualism Reconsidered*, pp. 17-25.

politan orbit.[24] "Life" as now lived anywhere is not good
enough, and the schools and those concerned with them
can hardly help but share in the task of inventing versions of urbanism we do not yet have—versions to stand,
as art and scientific endeavor do at their best, as pro-
jections beyond life rather than reflections and anticipa-
tions of it.

[24] This appears to be the recommendation of Professor Van
Cleve Morris in "The Other-Directed Man: Outline for a Recon-
structionist Philosophy of Man," *Teachers College Record*, vol. 57
(1956), pp. 238–240.

EPILOGUE

As I was working on these lectures, I was reading two very different documents. One was the vivid account in Andrew D. White's autobiography of the founding of Cornell—the brave battle that Ezra Cornell, and White with him, waged against sectarian, sectional (within New York), and simply corrupt or demagogic opposition. It is a tale of the triumph of good will over ill will, of enlightenment over obscurantism; almost a cops-and-robbers story in its shining simplicity. White tells how, agreeing with Herbert Spencer that he didn't want "mandarinism," or all universities to look alike, he had to fight for the admission of women to Cornell, and that when the first young women came, many men resigned, feeling their institution downgraded, though of course eventually the women proved an attraction and the Cornell model spread.

The other document was the account already referred to of the plight of school superintendents in New England (from the Harvard School of Education Executive Studies). These superintendents face today, from their school boards and parents and pressure groups, much the same sort of opposition that Cornell had to cope with: they are pressured to appoint local girls as teachers, to throw contracts to school board members' friends, to fire teachers for classroom views; their professionalism and that of their teachers is given but scant respect. Indeed, a university professor such as myself—whatever he may have to fear from the press or political attack—can scarcely imagine the degrading situation of exposure to certain school boards, for trustees often remain for a professor but shadowy and very generalized figures; moreover, they seldom run for election to represent an ethnic group, a part of town, a building lobby, or a taxpayers' league, nor is their turnover as rapid as many school boards'. The superintendents—many of whom began their careers as coaches or athletic directors—do not, however, respond to these attacks with the calm fortitude and faith in right reason of Ezra Cornell; they are depressed and feel harried on all sides; they keep looking around for a school board that will protect rather than chivvy them; and often, when they can, they get into other work. Ezra Cornell was wholly convinced that better education was the most important contribution he could make to his State, but the school superintendents on the other hand often feel more like overworked janitors than like educators. Yet with these superintendents (and with the high school teachers my students and colleagues have studied[1]) there appears to be a residual and often sardonically repressed idealism that helps

---

[1] These studies show that even a low level teachers college turns out idealistic graduates who are prepared to make many more demands on their profession than the settings they begin in will often allow. John Winget, who studied teachers in the Chicago schools under Professor Hughes' direction, found that the neophyte was likely to begin in the slum schools, which seniority had allowed the older teachers to escape from, save for those of the older teachers whom no other school principal would accept or who themselves preferred the routine horror to the unfamiliar challenge. This was like sending the greenest troops into the hottest combat in the care of a cadre of cynical corporals.

keep them going—an idealism that generally goes underground with the first experiences of a mean-spirited board or community or a hostile classroom.

Unfortunately, in many communities such experiences are frequent. Yet there are other communities where PTA groups and superintendents have combined to pull a whole school system out of torpor and defeatism. It was hard in the 1860s when the Cornell University battle was under way to imagine what the eventual fruits of the Morrill Act would be; and it is hard now to imagine what the high schools might be like several generations hence when, all the community having poured through them and scored its social-class and ethnic points, the superintendent's present perils might seem as remote as those Andrew White recounts.

It is fashionable today to sneer at the idea of progress as an illusion, fit only for an adolescent, Deweyan America, not a mature one which understands original sin and the dead weight of institutions. It is admittedly difficult to find unequivocal indices for progress, but I think it capricious to deny the possibility of it. Clearly, in the area of political control over colleges and schools, there has been progress of a sort: some professional standards have been set and frequently met; layers of administrative and institutional protection have been inserted between teachers and the corrupt or xenophobic elements in the community; and while these layers all too often give way under pressure, there is at least some professional consensus about minima of decency. And it is my impression that, taking the country as a whole, there is more academic freedom now, despite the terrible recent encroachments and the slow erosions of the public relations mentality, than there was a generation ago (a conclusion similar to that independently reached by Professor John P. Roche for civil liberties as a whole, as reported in a series of *New Republic* articles).[2]

One can look, moreover, at social control as well as political control—at the whole quality of faculty and student life—and see some signs of progress. In *The Bent Twig*, a novel of state university life published in 1915, Dorothy Canfield Fisher, daughter of a former professor at the University of Kansas, later Chancellor of Nebraska, describes the life of the beautiful, gifted, and athletic daughter of a professor, who is snubbed by the sororities when she enters the University where her father teaches. Wounded and lonely, she discovers her rejection is because her parents lead what we would today call an "exurban" life on the outskirts of the college town, where they enjoy chamber music, do-it-yourself activities, lack of swank, and the company of an ironical colleague who bears some resemblance to Veblen[3]—whereas they should properly live on a good downtown street, employ servants and go into debt, and cultivate the company of stuffy local businessmen and their genteel-aspiring wives. Veblen's own picture of the constricting social life he observed at the University of Missouri in Columbia is refracted in many of his comments on the American small town as well as in his discussion of pecuniary dominance over the universities in *The Higher Learning in America*. Although we can still find colleges as governed by convention and Chamber of Commerce values as those pictured by Veblen and Dor-

---

[2] Some anxiety in a teacher concerning his classroom conduct or writing is a sign of life—less depressing than the lack of it in those colleges where the professors are far too browbeaten to have anything to be scared about. Thus, there is more apprehension at the head of the procession where there is more freedom than at the tail where there is less.

[3] Mrs. Fisher kindly informs me that Veblen was not the model—there wasn't any particular one—for her portrait of professorial unconventionality.

othy Canfield Fisher, novelists today are not apt to teach there or otherwise to dig them out. Instead, the avant-garde books that satirize our academic life—recall Mary McCarthy's *The Groves of Academe* or Randall Jarrell's *Pictures at an Institution*—take for granted and even ridicule, because they are so widespread, those very "pastoral" attitudes that for Veblen or the family in *The Bent Twig* meant ostracism. While at Kansas or Missouri, one can very likely still find sorority snobbery and constriction among the students (as one can at other leading schools), the sorts of faculty gentility and wariness that Veblen and Dorothy Canfield Fisher write of could only be found there as vestiges; such universities have their accepted and respected Bohemians, awaiting a sardonic novelist.

As I say, I feel there is progress in these shifts. But since each level of cultural advance creates unforeseen problems and requires the invention of new forms of pioneering, those who comprise the avant-garde of the educational procession are dissatisfied and, if they look only to themselves, doubt that there is progress. It is in some ways like the situation which faces the socialists of Britain or Scandinavia: issues which, for such very different men as Andrew White and Veblen, were fighting issues have been won or bypassed or gone stale. What is left to be done—even if it is so enormous a task as bringing to the secondary schools and oppressed colleges the most thinly rationed models of excellence—can be felt (like the elimination of residual poverty in Sweden) as after all a mopping-up operation.

And there is no doubt that if the avant-garde long loses its momentum, the rest of the procession will eventually slow down. Freedom for the avant-garde to create new educational models is thus essential, but freedom is not enough without the confidence that education matters, and that not all ideas are already in the hands of veto groups.

Paradoxically, the avant-garde attack on John Dewey is beginning to coalesce into such a veto group itself. The young are told that Dewey is a naïve, overoptimistic, shallow, manipulative fellow, and (despite his neglected *A Common Faith*) without religious feeling. He lived too long, perhaps, to make "rediscovery" of him an immediate prospect, but I would regret it if people stopped reading him because of the prevailing legend as to the kind of thinker he was. Indeed, the attack on him is now so strong that, in many of the "backward countries" of American education, the adversaries arrive before Dewey himself, with the resulting reinforcement of old constraints which in these places need to be shaken loose. On the other hand, at the head of the procession, the changes both in our life and in our institutions of learning since Dewey wrote *The School and Society* in 1899 are such that the life outside, which he wanted to let inside, may mesh already too fully into our schools and colleges, thereby curbing their role as centers of countervailing power and bringing the status quo upon the new generation all too rapidly.

ANCHOR BOOKS